Breeding Landbird Monitoring

Northeast Temperate Network 2008 Annual Report

Natural Resource Report NPS/NETN/NRR—2009/105

Steven D. Faccio
Vermont Center for Ecostudies
20 Palmer Court
White River Junction, VT 05001

Brian R. Mitchell
Northeast Temperate Network
National Park Service
54 Elm Street
Woodstock, VT 05091

May 2009

U.S. Department of the Interior
National Park Service
Natural Resource Program Center
Fort Collins, Colorado

The Natural Resource Publication series addresses natural resource topics that are of interest and applicability to a broad readership in the National Park Service and to others in the management of natural resources, including the scientific community, the public, and the NPS conservation and environmental constituencies. Manuscripts are peer-reviewed to ensure that the information is scientifically credible, technically accurate, appropriately written for the intended audience, and is designed and published in a professional manner.

Natural Resource Reports are the designated medium for disseminating high priority, current natural resource management information with managerial application. The series targets a general, diverse audience, and may contain NPS policy considerations or address sensitive issues of management applicability. Examples of the diverse array of reports published in this series include vital signs monitoring plans; monitoring protocols; "how to" resource management papers; proceedings of resource management workshops or conferences; annual reports of resource programs or divisions of the Natural Resource Program Center; resource action plans; fact sheets; and regularly-published newsletters.

Views, statements, findings, conclusions, recommendations and data in this report are solely those of the author(s) and do not necessarily reflect views and policies of the U.S. Department of the Interior, NPS. Mention of trade names or commercial products does not constitute endorsement or recommendation for use by the National Park Service.

This report is available from the Northeast Temperate Network website (http://science.nature.nps.gov/im/units/netn/) and the Natural Resource Publications Management website (http://www.nature.nps.gov/publications/NRPM).

Please cite this publication as:

Faccio, S. D., and B. R. Mitchell. 2009. Breeding landbird monitoring: Northeast Temperate Network 2008 annual report. Natural Resource Report NPS/NETN/NRR—2009/105. National Park Service, Fort Collins, Colorado.

NPS D-57 May 2009

Contents

Figures

Tables

Acknowledgments

The success of the Northeast Temperate Network (NETN) Landbird Monitoring Program depends on the generosity of project volunteers, whose data this report is based upon. We extend our sincere thanks to the 21 volunteers listed below, who crawled out of bed at ungodly hours, endured hordes of biting mosquitoes and blackflies, and contributed their time, efforts, and expert birding skills.

Peg Ackerson
Thom Almendinger
Tom Bjorkman
Sherrie Downing
Pat Fitzgerald
Jason Forbes
Ted Gaine
Leda Beth Gray
Lora Haller
Julie Hart
Dave Hayes
Andy Lamy
Randolph Little
Richard MacDonald
Kent McFarland
Matthew Medler
Ben Olewine
Kelly Perkins
James Restivo
Tom Sharp
Tim Spahr

Introduction

The Northeast Temperate Network (NETN) of the National Park Service is tasked with monitoring a suite of representative indicators, called vital signs, of natural resource condition for 12 parks in seven northeastern states and the Appalachian NST. Breeding birds were chosen as one of the NETN vital signs because they are a reliable indicator of ecosystem integrity and they are a high profile taxonomic group. Birds are also easily detected and identified, and well-established survey methods are available. This report pertains only to breeding bird monitoring in 11 of the NETN parks (Figure 1).

The Northeast Temperate Network and the Vermont Center for Ecostudies (VCE) began monitoring breeding birds in most network parks in 2006, using volunteer birders to conduct point count surveys. On a broad scale, all 11 parks are located within the temperate deciduous forest biome. At a finer scale, the parks range across four Bird Conservation Regions (BCRs) (Figure 1). Bird Conservation Regions, developed by the North American Bird Conservation Initiative (NABCI 2000), are ecologically defined units that provide a consistent spatial framework for bird conservation across North American landscapes. By employing broad scale units that are ecologically meaningful to bird populations, conservation efforts can be tailored to support groups of species throughout the heart of their ranges. Bird Conservation Regions are being used to help assign "conservation priority" scores for bird species. Each BCR has its own unique list of "priority" species ranked by conservation importance according to a standardized set of criteria.

This report summarizes data collected in 2007 and 2008. The 2006 data is being converted and imported into the current program database, and will be included in future annual reports. We also plan to expand this report in upcoming years to incorporate more interpretation of the results. For now, please keep in mind that some differences between the two years are due to differences in the number of sites and points surveyed in each park. In addition, readers should treat the index of biological integrity (IBI) results as provisional. There are two reasons for this: 1) the IBI assumes that the bird community is completely characterized, and if a subset of species are rare and hard to detect the results could be biased; and 2) many NETN parks have a primary mandate to manage for the historical landscape rather than biological integrity or ecosystem structure and function; thus, management action may not always be warranted when guilds are rated "significant concern". We hope to address both of these issues in the next year or two by exploring the value of combining data from multiple years when constructing the IBI, and by working with park managers to produce a parallel IBI based on park management goals.

Methods

Depending on size and habitat, each park contains one or more study sites with 3-12 point count locations, each separated by 250 m. Volunteer birders visit each point at least once per year between late May and June; parks with fewer than 10 point count locations are visited multiple times. Volunteers record the species of each individual they detect, the time during the count when each individual is first detected, and the distance band within which each individual was detected (0-10 m, 10-25 m, 25-50 m, and >50 m). The data are recorded on field cards and input into the USGS Point Count Database, which was first used for archiving data in 2007. Data from 2006 surveys have yet to be incorporated into the USGS Point Count Database, and therefore results from that year do not appear in this report.

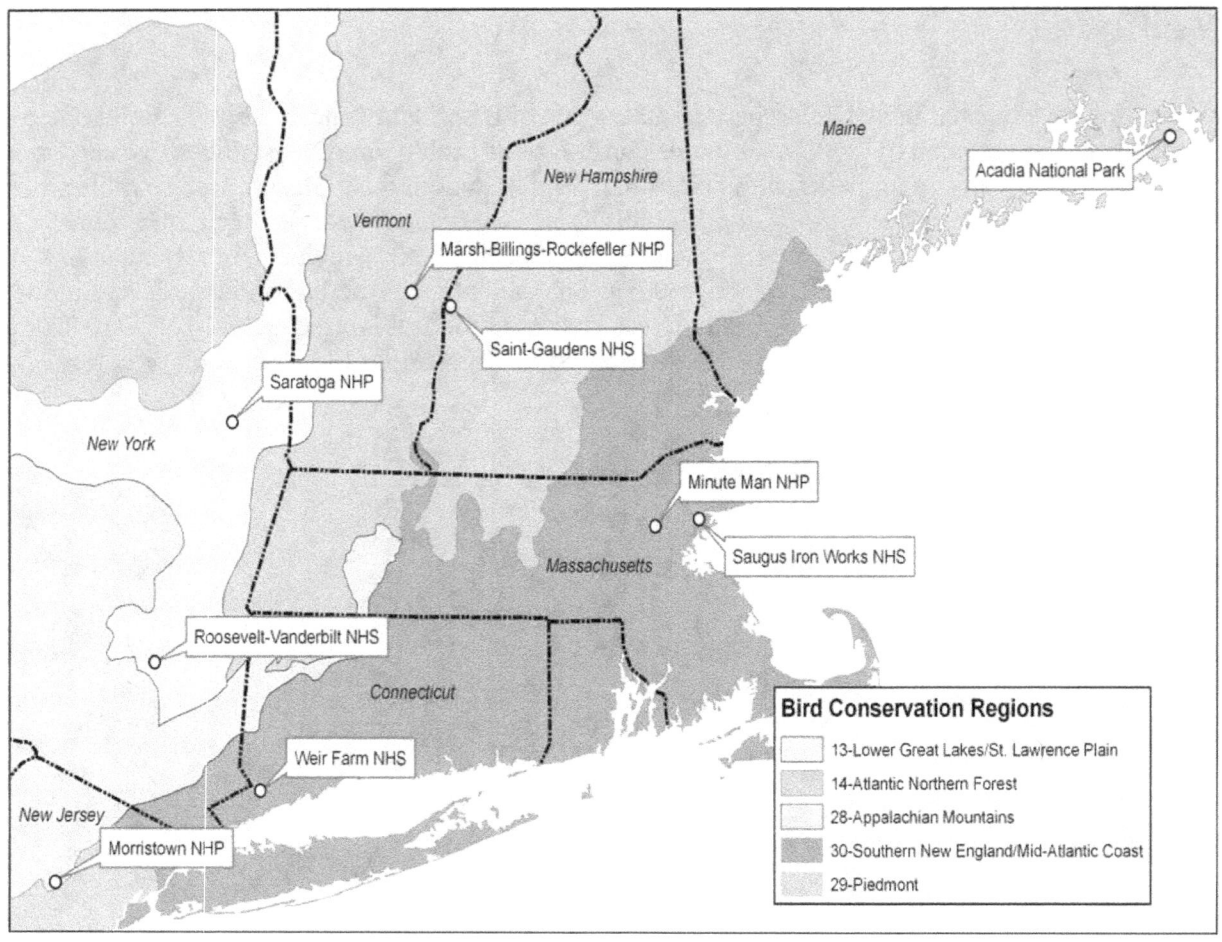

Figure 1. Northeast Temperate Network parks where the breeding bird monitoring protocol is being implemented and their associated Bird Conservation Regions. Roosevelt-Vanderbilt National Historical Site includes Eleanor Roosevelt, Home of Franklin D. Roosevelt, and Vanderbilt Mansion National Historical Sites.

Index of Biotic Integrity

Included in this summary is an assessment of the biotic integrity of the forest breeding bird community at each park based on an assemblage of behavioral and physiological response guilds (i.e., groups of species that require similar habitat, food, or other elements for survival). Such an index of biotic integrity (IBI) will help elucidate changes in a broader, landscape context and indicate in which direction breeding bird habitat at the park may be moving along a disturbance gradient from "highly disturbed" or "urban," to "pristine" or "natural."

The guild-based avian integrity scorecard consists of 13 guilds in eight guild categories, with each guild being broadly categorized as "specialist" or "generalist." A specialist can be a species with a narrow range of habitat tolerances, or one that exhibits a low intrinsic rate of population growth. Specialist guilds may be thought of as those indicative of a high-integrity habitat condition, while generalist guilds are those indicative of a low-integrity condition.

To calculate the IBI, species are first assigned to guilds (some species may be assigned to more than one guild, depending on their life history traits). The proportional species richness of each guild is then calculated by dividing the number of guild members detected by the total number of species detected. This value is then used to determine a rank of "Good", "Caution", or "Significant Concern" based on the proportional species richness thresholds and ranks listed in Table 1. "Good" represents acceptable or desired conditions; "Caution" indicates a problem may exist; "Significant concern" indicates undesired conditions that may be in need of management actions. For grasslands at Saratoga National Historical Park, we have also developed a grassland bird assessment, based on a small number of guilds relevant to grasslands (Table 2).

The thresholds and ranks are largely based on those derived by O'Connell et al. (2000) for birds in forested habitats in the central Appalachians, and from those derived by Glennon and Porter (2005) for New York's Adirondack State Park. The thresholds and ranks for grassland birds were derived from Browder et al. (2002) and Coppedge et al. (2006). This is a first attempt at applying this index; threshold values may need to be adjusted by bioregion, forest type or BCR, and may also be refined over time. In addition, some guild members were likely missed during surveys, so readers should not be concerned about low ratings presented in this report unless most of the metrics are on the lower range within a category for multiple years. We also recognize that this scorecard is based on ecological criteria, and that park management goals may not seek to attain ecological integrity, as defined for the IBI. A management scorecard could be developed by park staff and NETN scientists that would reflect progress towards avian and ecological management goals for individual parks.

For more information about the Avian Index of Biotic Integrity, as well as project methodologies, sampling scheme, etc, see the Breeding Landbird Monitoring Protocol (Faccio et al. 2009), available at the NPS Northeast Temperate Network website at http://science.nature.nps.gov/im/units/NETN/monitor/.

Table 1. Avian Integrity Ranks for 13 response guilds and proportional species richness thresholds (based on O'Connell et al. 2000, and Glennon and Porter 2005).

Biotic Integrity Element	Response Guild Metric (Percent Species Richness)	Ratings		
		Good	Caution	Significant Concern
Compositional:	Exotic Species	0%	0.5-7%	>7%
	Nest Predators/Brood Parasite	<10%	10-15%	>15%
	Residents	<28%	28-41%	>41%
	Single Brooded	>68%	50-68%	<50%
Functional:	Bark Prober	>11%	4-11%	<4%
	Ground Gleaner	>9%	4-9%	<4%
	High Canopy Forager	>12%	7-12%	<7%
	Low Canopy Forager	>22%	14-22%	<14%
	Omnivore	<30%	30-50%	>50%
Structural:	Canopy Nester	>35%	29-35%	<29%
	Forest-ground Nester	>18%	5-18%	<5%
	Interior Forest Obligate	>35%	10-35%	<10%
	Shrub Nester	<18%	18-24%	>24%

Table 2. Avian Integrity Ranks for four response guilds and proportional species richness thresholds (based on Browder et al. (2002) and Coppedge et al. (2006)

Response Guild Metric (Percent Species Richness)	Ratings		
	Good	Caution	Significant Concern
Edge generalist species	<20%	20-50%	>50%
Shrub-dependant species	<10%	10-25%	>25%
Grassland obligate species	>10%	5-10%	<5%
Exotic species	0%	0.1%-3%	>3%

Results by Park

Acadia National Park (Maine)

A total of 51 point count locations in seven study sites were established in 2007 at Acadia National Park (ACAD) (Maine). Of these, three sites on Mt. Desert Island (MDI) were surveyed in 2007 and 2008 (Figure 2). One site on the Schoodic Peninsula that was surveyed in 2007 was not sampled in 2008 (Figure 3). On MDI, point counts were conducted at the Giant Slide Trail (n=10 points), Seal Cove East (n=7 points), and Seal Cove Center (n=6 points); the Seal Cove sites were surveyed twice.

A total of 262 birds were detected in 2007, and 333 birds were detected in 2008 (including repeat site visits). Forty-five total species were recorded, including the Yellow-Bellied Sapsucker and Eastern Phoebe, which were detected on the second survey in 2008. There was an average abundance of 9.83 birds per point (excluding the second survey). Four species of regional conservation concern were detected during the surveys: Boreal Chickadee, Wood Thrush, Blackpoll Warbler, and Eastern Towhee. Appendices A and B contain the species and relative abundances found throughout the park and at each site during the first survey of each year, and other summary statistics. At all sites combined in 2008, seven of the 10 most abundant species were above 2007 levels, while three were below (Figure 4).

The park-wide IBI results for Acadia National Park changed in rating for three guilds between 2007 and 2008, and the presence of only one guild with a rating of "Significant Concern" indicates that the forest bird community is doing well (Table 3). The IBI has also been calculated for each site, and these results are in Appendix C.

Figure 2. Breeding landbird monitoring point count locations at Acadia National Park, Mt. Desert Island.

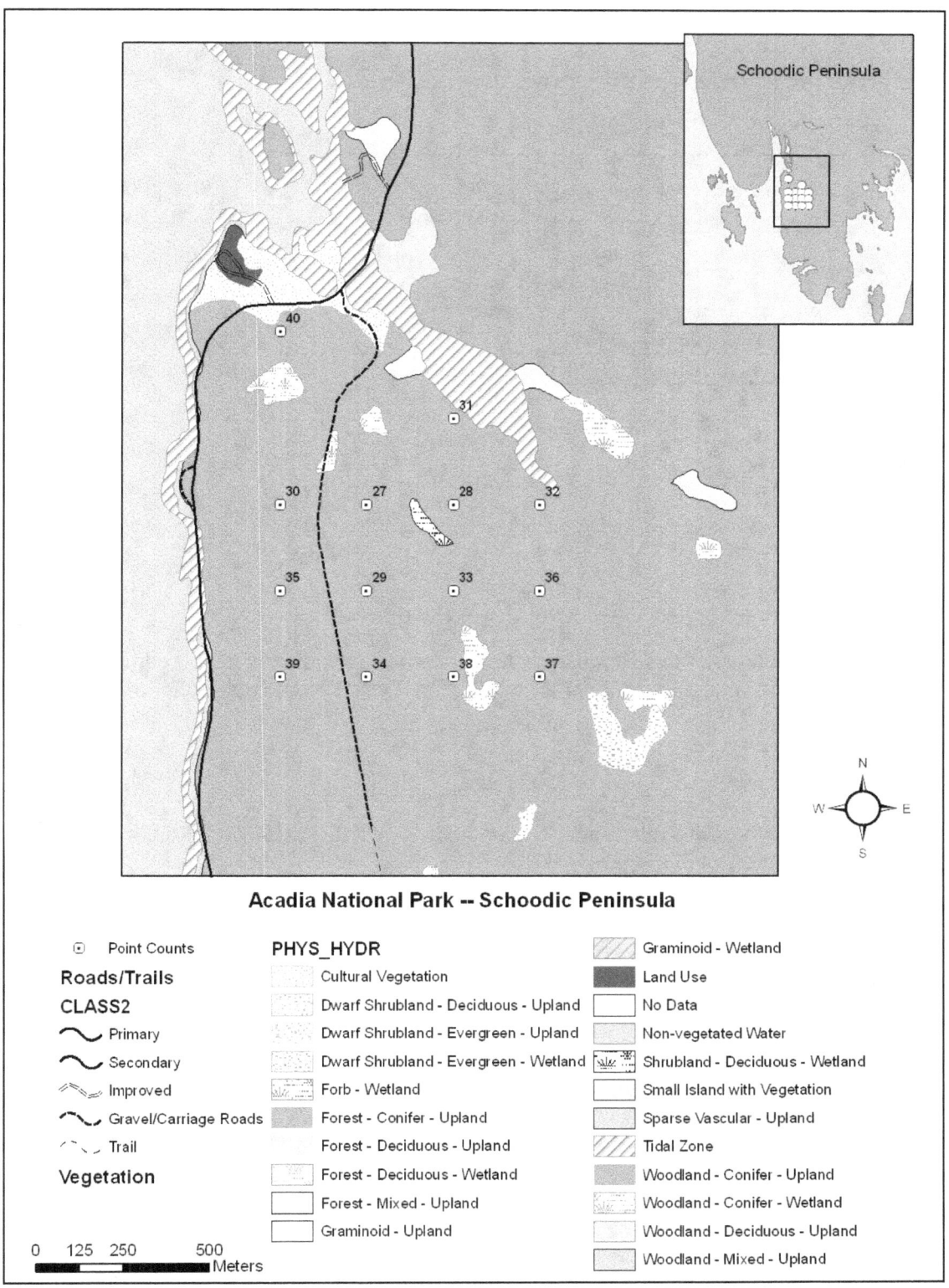

Figure 3. Breeding landbird monitoring point count locations at Acadia National Park, Schoodic Peninsula.

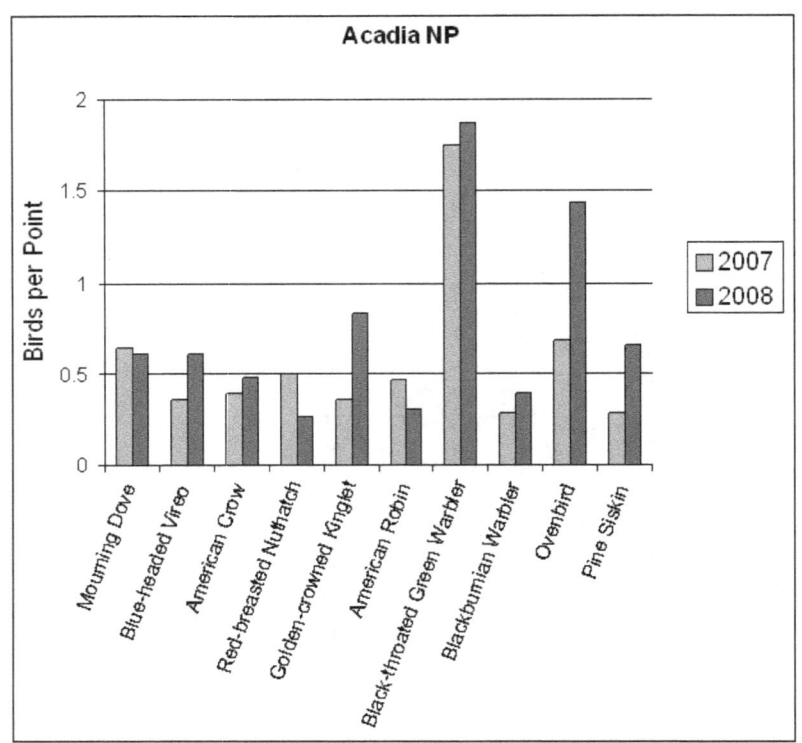

Figure 4. Relative abundance of the 10 most common species detected during breeding landbird monitoring at Acadia National Park in 2007 and 2008; Mt. Desert Island and Schoodic Peninsula sites.

Table 3. Index of Biotic Integrity for Acadia National Park for 2007 and 2008. Ranks that changed between years are in boldface.

		Percent Species Richness		Biotic Integrity Rating	
Response Guild		2007	2008	2007	2008
Composition:	Exotic	0%	0%	Good	Good
	Nest Pred / Brood Parasite	8%	9%	Good	Good
	Resident	33%	33%	Caution	Caution
	Single Brooded	56%	58%	Caution	Caution
Function:	Bark Prober	13%	12%	Good	Good
Ground	**Gleaner**	**8%**	**9%**	**Caution**	**Good**
	High Canopy Forager	8%	9%	Caution	Caution
	Low Canopy Forager	23%	24%	Good	Good
Om	**nivore**	**31%**	**27%**	**Caution**	**Good**
Structure:	Canopy Nester	36%	36%	Good	Good
	Forest-ground Nester	13%	12%	Caution	Caution
	Interior Forest Obligate	44%	45%	Good	Good
	Shrub Nester	**23%**	**24%**	**Caution**	**Sig Conc**

Eleanor Roosevelt National Historic Site (New York)

The Roosevelt-Vanderbilt National Historic Sites (ROVA) consist of three separate park units at which study sites were established and surveyed in 2006, 2007, and 2008. The study site at Eleanor Roosevelt NHS (ELRO) originally consisted of six point counts, but five additional sampling points were added for the 2007 field season, increasing the total to 11 point counts (Figure 5).

One hundred and thirteen individual birds were detected in 2007, and 82 birds were detected in 2008. In total, 32 species were recorded in both years, and there was an average abundance of 8.9 birds per point. In 2008, both relative abundance and species richness declined from 2007, despite several new species being encountered (Ruby-throated Hummingbird, Downy Woodpecker, Northern Flicker, and Black-Capped Chickadee). A total of four species of conservation concern were detected during 2007 and 2008: Eastern Wood-Pewee, Wood Thrush, Worm-Eating Warbler, and Baltimore Oriole. A list of species, their relative abundances, and other summary statistics are provided in Appendix A. Wood Thrush, Tufted Titmouse, and Northern Cardinal were the most commonly detected species (Figure 6).

The park-wide IBI results changed in rating for only one guild between 2007 and 2008; "resident" went from caution to significant concern. The park received an average rating of "Caution," perhaps indicative of its location on a fragmented landscape (Table 4).

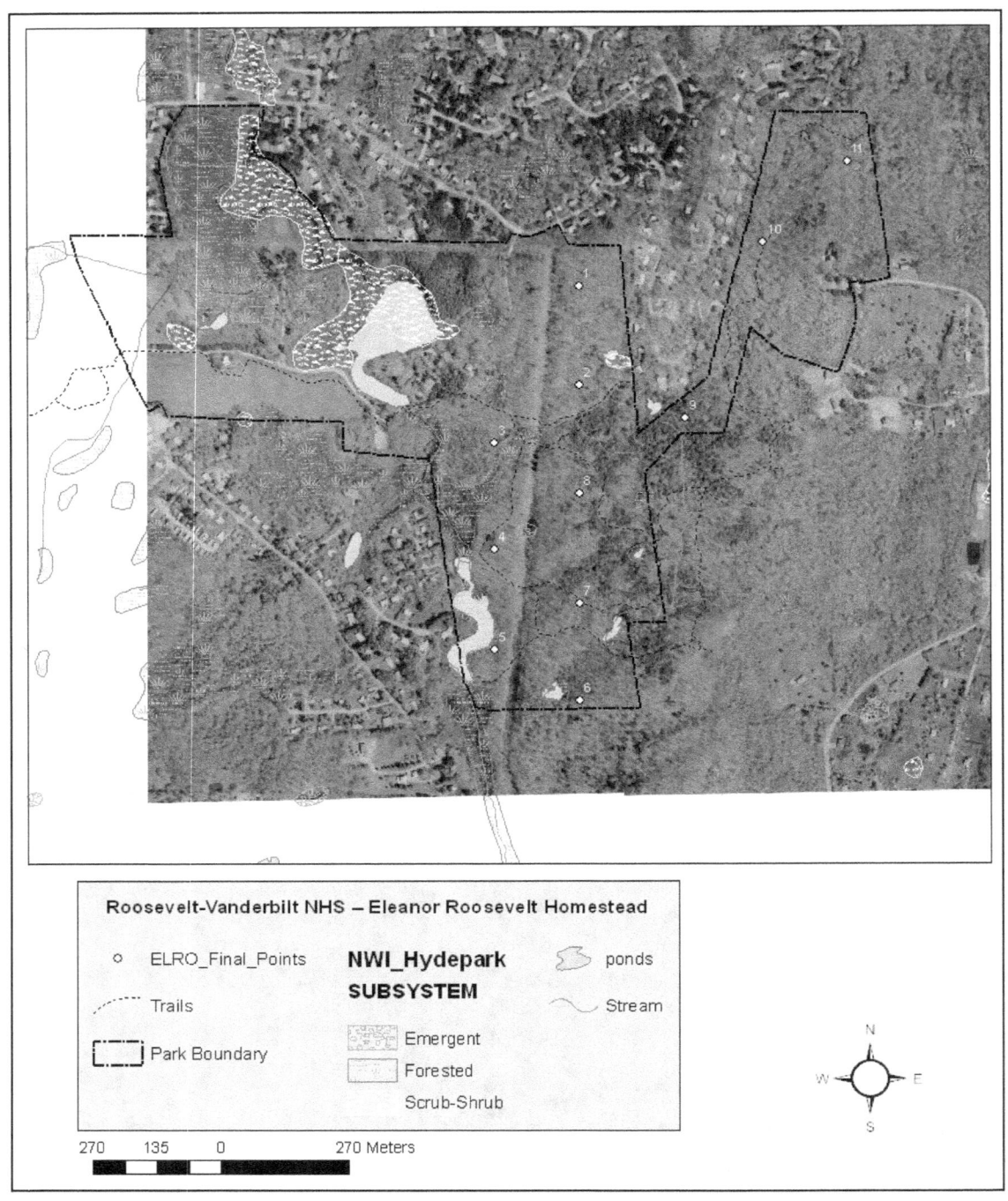

Figure 5. Breeding landbird monitoring point count locations at Eleanor Roosevelt National Historic Site.

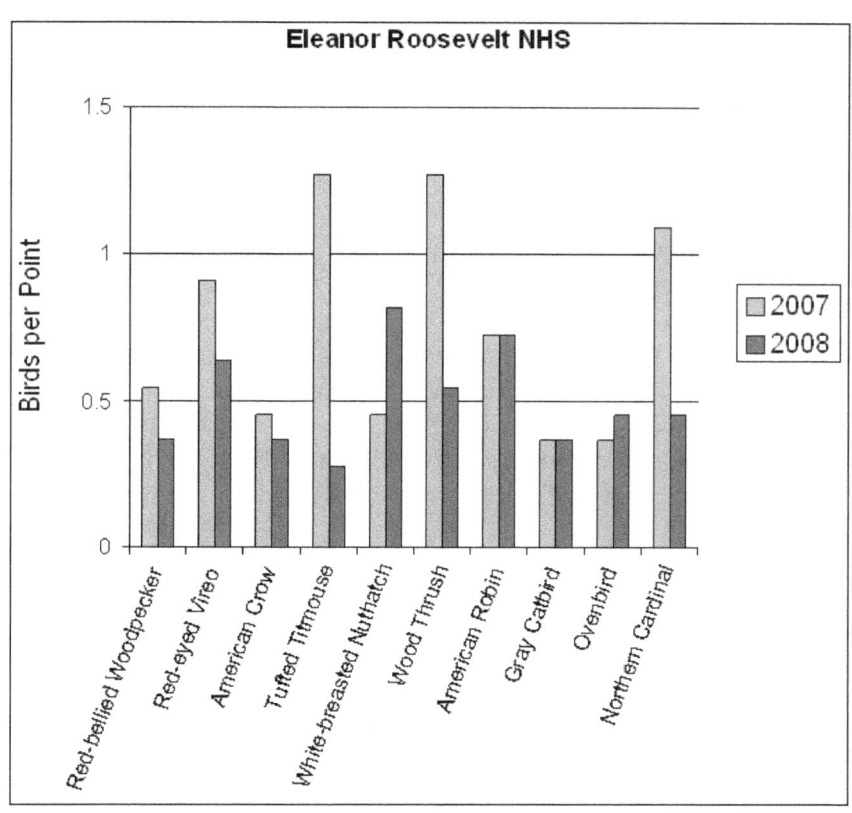

Figure 6. Relative abundance of the 10 most common species at Eleanor Roosevelt National Historic Site in 2007 and 2008.

Table 4. Index of Biotic Integrity for Eleanor Roosevelt National Historic Site for 2007 and 2008. Ranks that changed between years are in boldface.

		Percent Species Richness		Biotic Integrity Rating	
Response Guild		2007	2008	2007	2008
Composition:	Exotic	0%	0%	Good	Good
	Nest Pred / Brood Parasite	7%	9%	Good	Good
Resident		**36%**	**43%**	**Caution**	**Sig Conc**
	Single Brooded	46%	48%	Sig Conc	Sig Conc
Function:	Bark Prober	18%	22%	Good	Good
	Ground Gleaner	7%	9%	Caution	Caution
	High Canopy Forager	7%	9%	Caution	Caution
	Low Canopy Forager	0%	4%	Sig Conc	Sig Conc
	Omnivore	46%	43%	Caution	Caution
Structure:	Canopy Nester	25%	26%	Caution	Caution
	Forest-ground Nester	11%	9%	Caution	Caution
	Interior Forest Obligate	29%	26%	Caution	Caution
	Shrub Nester	25%	26%	Sig Conc	Sig Conc

13

Home of Franklin D. Roosevelt National Historic Site (New York)

The Roosevelt-Vanderbilt National Historic Sites (ROVA) consist of three separate park units at which study sites were established and surveyed in 2006, 2007, and 2008. Twelve point count locations were established at the Home of Franklin D. Roosevelt National Historic Sites (HOFR) (Figure 7).

A total of 101 birds were detected in 2007, and 83 birds were detected in 2008. In total, 36 species were recorded, and there was an average abundance of 7.7 birds per point. Both relative abundance and species richness declined between 2007 and 2008, despite several new species being encountered in 2008: Mute Swan, Northern Flicker, Yellow-Throated Vireo, American Crow, Brown Creeper, Carolina Wren, and Ovenbird. Three species of conservation concern were detected during 2007 and 2008 surveys: Eastern Wood-Pewee, Wood Thrush, and Baltimore Oriole. A list of species, their relative abundances, and other summary statistics are provided in Appendix A. Tufted Titmouse, Red-Eyed Vireo, and Wood Thrush were the most commonly detected species (Figure 8).

The park-wide IBI results changed in rating for several guilds between 2007 and 2008. This suggests that the species community was not characterized well enough for the IBI to be stable. The index assumes that all species that are present are detected, and if a number of species are present at very low abundances they will be detected in some years and not in others. This variation in whether species are detected can cause the IBI metrics to fluctuate between ratings, and in this situation combining data for multiple years may yield a more realistic assessment. The park received an average rating of "Caution," perhaps indicative of its location on a fragmented landscape (Table 5).

Figure 7. Breeding landbird monitoring point count locations at the Home of Franklin D. Roosevelt National Historic Site.

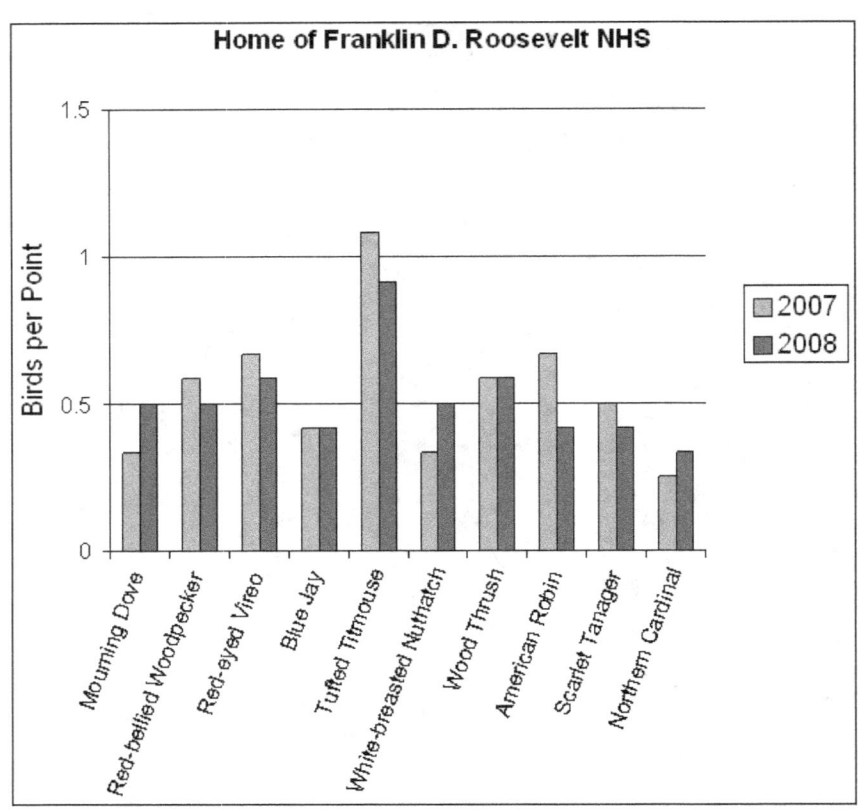

Figure 8. Relative abundance of the 10 most common species detected at the Home of Franklin D. Roosevelt National Historic Site in 2007 and 2008.

Table 5. Index of Biotic Integrity for the Home of Franklin D. Roosevelt National Historic Site for 2007 and 2008. Ranks that changed between years are in boldface.

		Percent Species Richness		Biotic Integrity Rating	
Response Guild		2007	2008	2007	2008
Composition:	Exotic	0%	0%	Good	Good
	Nest Pred / Brood Parasite	10%	13%	Caution	Caution
Resident		**34%**	**52%**	**Caution**	**Sig Conc**
	Single Brooded	48%	48%	Sig Conc	Sig Conc
Function:	Bark Prober	14%	22%	Good	Good
	Ground Gleaner	**0%**	**9%**	**Sig Conc**	**Caution**
	High Canopy Forager	10%	13%	Caution	Good
	Low Canopy Forager	10%	9%	Sig Conc	Sig Conc
Om	**nivore**	**34%**	**26%**	**Caution**	**Good**
Structure:	Canopy Nester	34%	30%	Caution	Caution
	Forest-ground Nester	**3%**	**9%**	**Sig Conc**	**Caution**
	Interior Forest Obligate	17%	26%	Caution	Caution
	Shrub Nester	**24%**	**17%**	**Sig Conc**	**Good**

Marsh-Billings-Rockefeller National Historical Park (Vermont)

Three study sites were established at the Marsh Billings-Rockefeller National Historical Park (MABI) and surveyed in 2006, 2007, and 2008. Two of these sites (MABI Northwest and MABI East) consist of 10 point counts each, and one site (MABI South) consists of five point counts (Figure 9). In 2008, only five of the 10 point counts at MABI Northwest were completed due to inclement weather, although those five points were surveyed twice.

A total of 407 individual birds were detected in 2007, and 351 birds were detected in 2008 (including the second survey of the Northwest site); 51 total species were recorded, with an average abundance of 14.7 birds per point (excluding the second survey). Despite three new species being encountered in 2008 (Chestnut-sided Warbler, Cedar Waxwing, and Wild Turkey), both total abundance and species richness declined. Two species of regional conservation concern, Wood Thrush and Bobolink, were detected during the surveys. A list of species, their relative abundances, and other summary statistics are provided in Appendices A and B. Ovenbird and Red-eyed Vireo were the most abundant species detected (Figure 10).

The park-wide IBI rating for Marsh-Billings-Rockefeller National Historic Park only changed for two guilds between 2007 and 2008, and the lack of any guilds with a rating of "Significant Concern" indicates that the forest breeding bird community is doing well (Table 6). The IBI has also been calculated for each site, individually, and these results are provided in Appendix C.

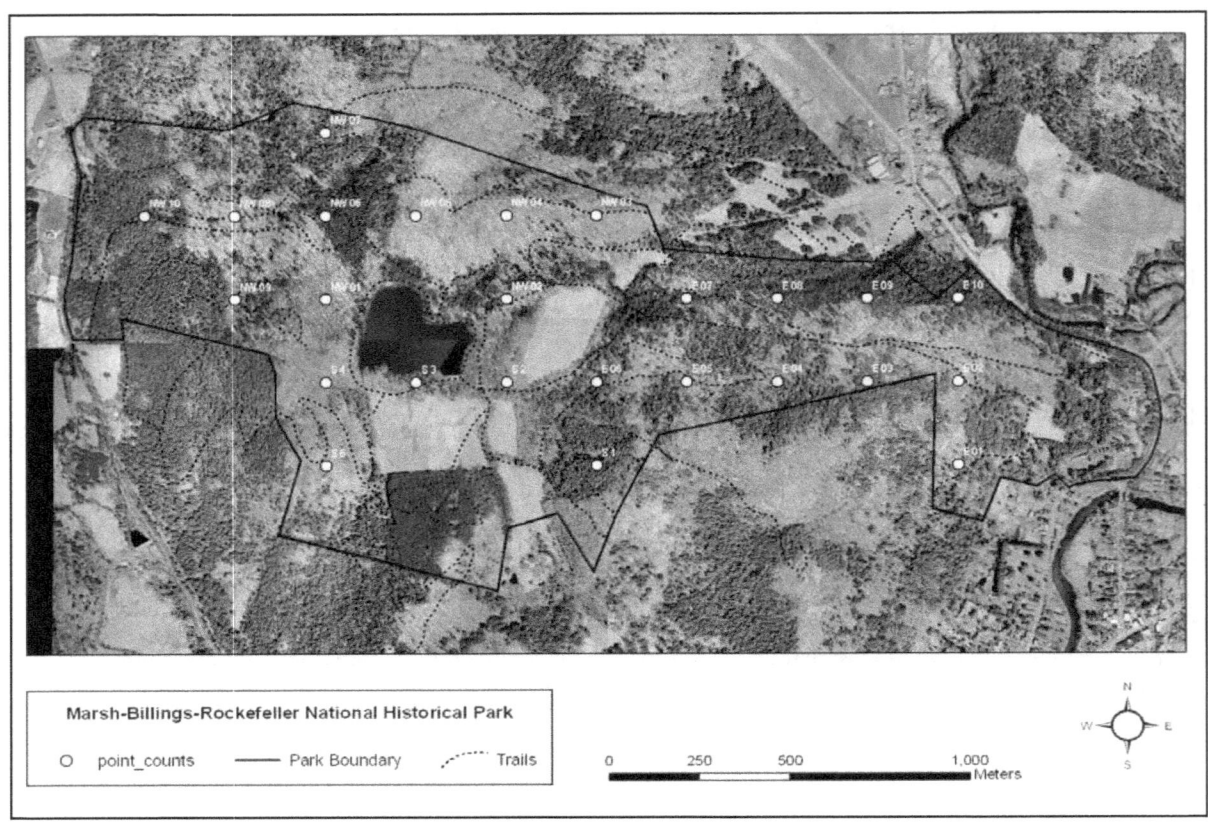

Figure 9. Breeding landbird monitoring point count locations at Marsh-Billings-Rockefeller National Historical Park.

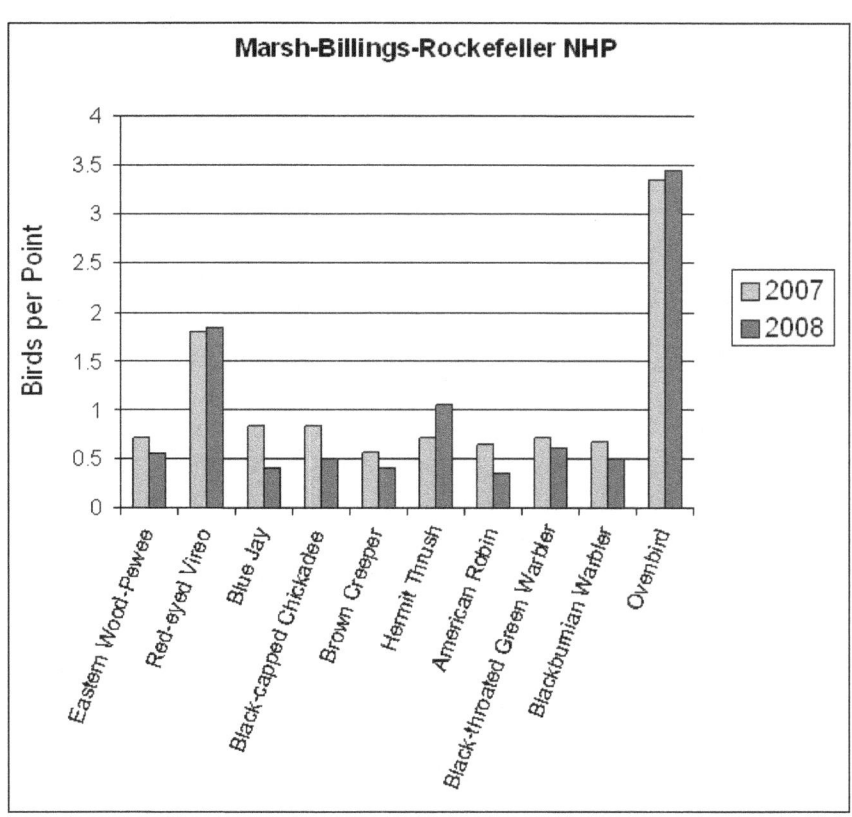

Figure 10. Relative abundance of the 10 most common species detected at Marsh-Billings-Rockefeller National Historic Park in 2007 and 2008.

Table 6. Index of Biotic Integrity for Marsh-Billings-Rockefeller National Historic Park for 2007 and 2008. Ranks that changed between years are in boldface.

		Percent Species Richness		Biotic Integrity Rating	
Response Guild		2007	2008	2007	2008
Composition:	Exotic	0%	0%	Good	Good
	Nest Pred / Brood Parasite	**6%**	**10%**	**Good**	**Caution**
Resident		**27%**	**28%**	**Good**	**Caution**
	Single Brooded	54%	56%	Caution	Caution
Function:	Bark Prober	17%	13%	Good	Good
	Ground Gleaner	8%	8%	Caution	Caution
	High Canopy Forager	8%	10%	Caution	Caution
	Low Canopy Forager	15%	18%	Caution	Caution
	Omnivore	31%	33%	Caution	Caution
Structure:	Canopy Nester	35%	38%	Good	Good
	Forest-ground Nester	13%	10%	Caution	Caution
	Interior Forest Obligate	40%	36%	Good	Good
	Shrub Nester	19%	23%	Caution	Caution

Minute Man National Historical Park (Massachusetts)

Three study sites were established at the Minute Man National Historical Park (MIMA) and were surveyed in 2006, 2007, and 2008. Two of these sites (The Bluff and Miriam's Corner) consisted of 8 point counts each, and one site (Hartwell Tavern) consisted of seven point counts (Figure 11). The Bluff was surveyed twice in both years.

A total of 384 individual birds were detected in 2007, and 347 birds were detected in 2008 (including repeat surveys). Forty-six species were recorded, including a Wild Turkey that was seen on a repeat survey of The Bluff in 2008, and there was an average abundance of 12.2 birds per point (excluding the repeat survey). Despite several new species being encountered in 2008, total abundance declined and species richness was relatively stable. A total of eight species of regional conservation concern were detected during the two survey years, including four species that were detected in both years (Eastern Wood-Pewee, Wood Thrush, Scarlet Tanager, and Rose-Breasted Grosbeak). A list of species, their relative abundances, and other summary statistics for the first survey of each point are provided in Appendices A and B. Tufted Titmouse, American Robin, and Blue Jay were the most abundant species detected (Figure 12).

The park-wide IBI for Minute Man National Historical Park rating shifted for only two guilds between 2007 and 2008, and the presence of numerous "Significant Concern" ratings and few "Good" ratings is likely due to the urbanized and highly fragmented landscape of the park (Table 7). The IBI has also been calculated for each site, and these results are in Appendix C.

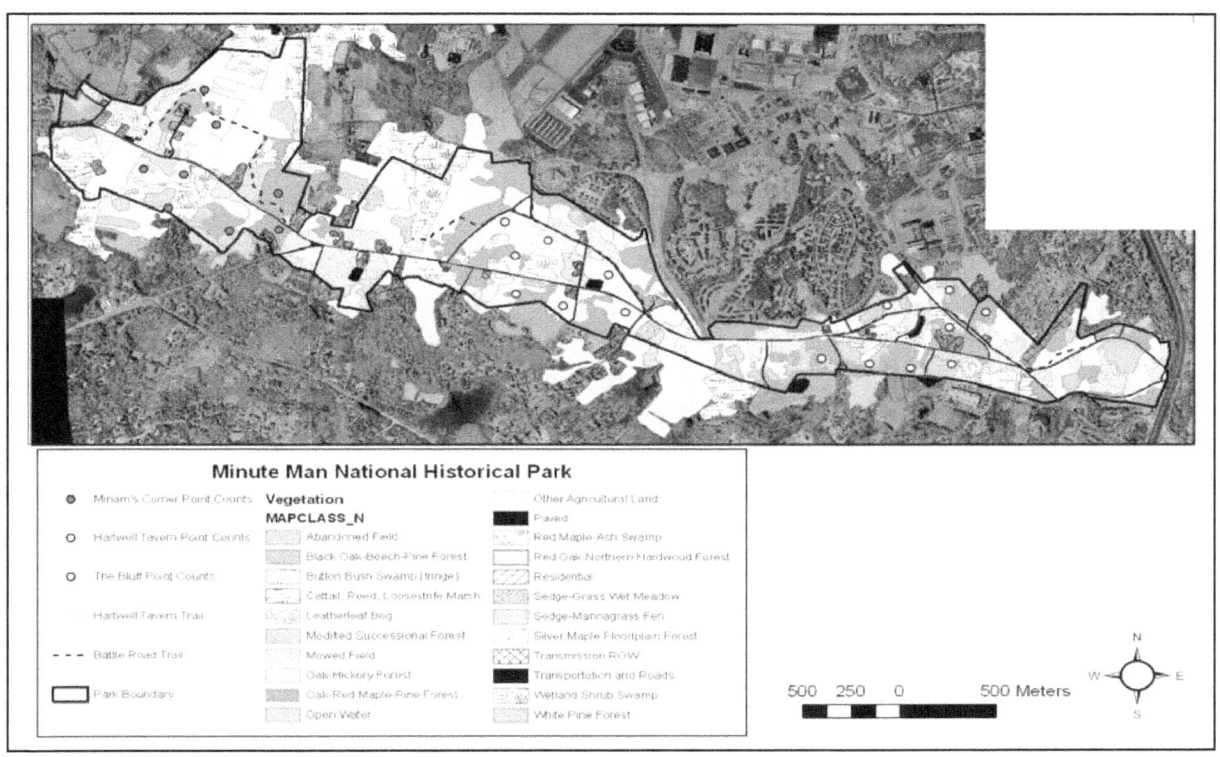

Figure 11. Breeding landbird monitoring point count locations at Minute Man National Historical Park.

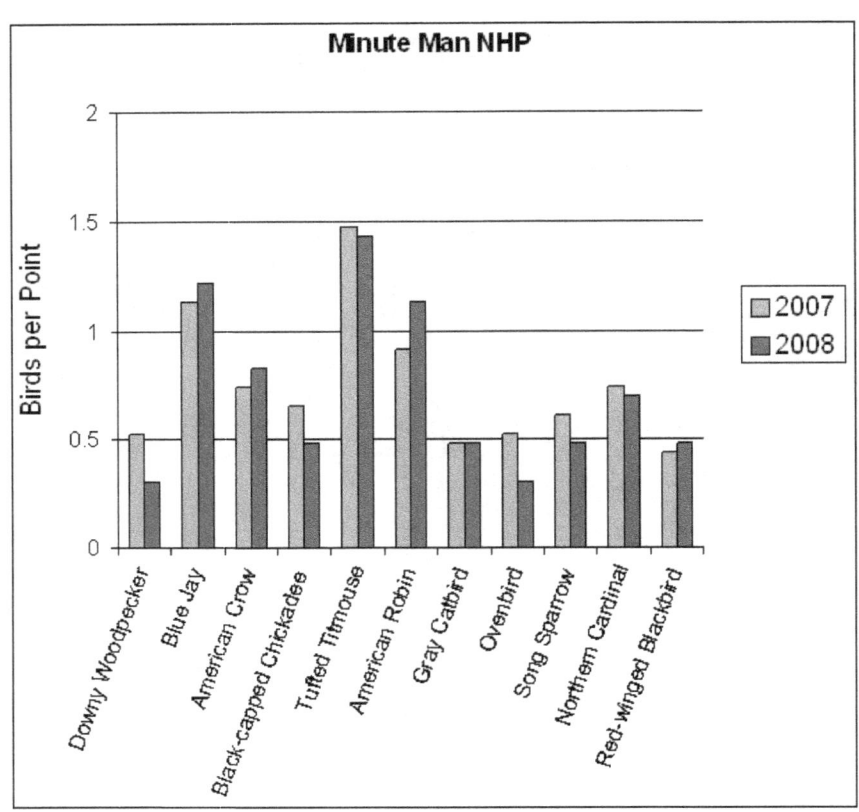

Figure 12. Relative abundance of the 11 most common species detected at Minute Man National Historic Park in 2007 and 2008.

Table 7. Index of Biotic Integrity for Minute Man National Historic Park for 2007 and 2008. Ranks that changed between years are in boldface.

Response Guild		Percent Species Richness		Biotic Integrity Rating	
		2007	2008	2007	2008
Composition:	Exotic	5%	6%	Caution	Caution
	Nest Pred / Brood Parasite	8%	8%	Good	Good
	Resident	38%	31%	Caution	Caution
	Single Brooded	38%	36%	Sig Conc	Sig Conc
Function:	Bark Prober	13%	11%	Good	Good
	Ground Gleaner	5%	6%	Caution	Caution
	High Canopy Forager	**5%**	**8%**	**Sig Conc**	**Caution**
	Low Canopy Forager	13%	11%	Sig Conc	Sig Conc
	Omnivore	44%	42%	Caution	Caution
Structure:	Canopy Nester	26%	22%	Caution	Caution
	Forest-ground Nester	**5%**	**3%**	**Caution**	**Sig Conc**
	Interior Forest Obligate	18%	11%	Caution	Caution
	Shrub Nester	28%	33%	Sig Conc	Sig Conc

22

Morristown National Historical Park (New Jersey)

Three study sites were established at the Morristown National Historical Park (MORR), two of which (Primrose Brook and Soldier's Huts) were surveyed in 2006 and 2007, and two (Primrose Brook and Mt. Kemble) were surveyed in 2008. Primrose Brook and Mt. Kemble consisted of 10 point counts each, while Soldier's Huts consisted of nine point counts (Figure 13). Mt. Kemble was surveyed twice in 2008.

A total of 261 individual birds were detected in 2007, and 442 birds were detected in 2008 (including the repeat survey). Forty-two total species were recorded, including an American Goldfinch detected on the repeat survey of Mt. Kemble, and there was an average abundance of 12.5 birds per point (excluding the repeat survey). A total of seven species of regional conservation concern were detected during the two survey years, including two species, Wood Thrush and Eastern Wood-Pewee, that were among the ten most abundant species detected (Figure 14). A list of species, their relative abundances, and other summary statistics from the first survey of each point are provided in Appendices A and B. Wood Thrush and Blue Jay were the most abundant species detected (Figure 14).

The park-wide IBI rating changed for three guilds between 2007 and 2008. While the composition metrics were generally "Good," structure and function metrics were often "Caution." This could be related to the low structural diversity in much of the park; the legacy of a high deer population has resulted in very limited forest regeneration (Table 8). The IBI has also been calculated for each site, and these results are provided in Appendix C.

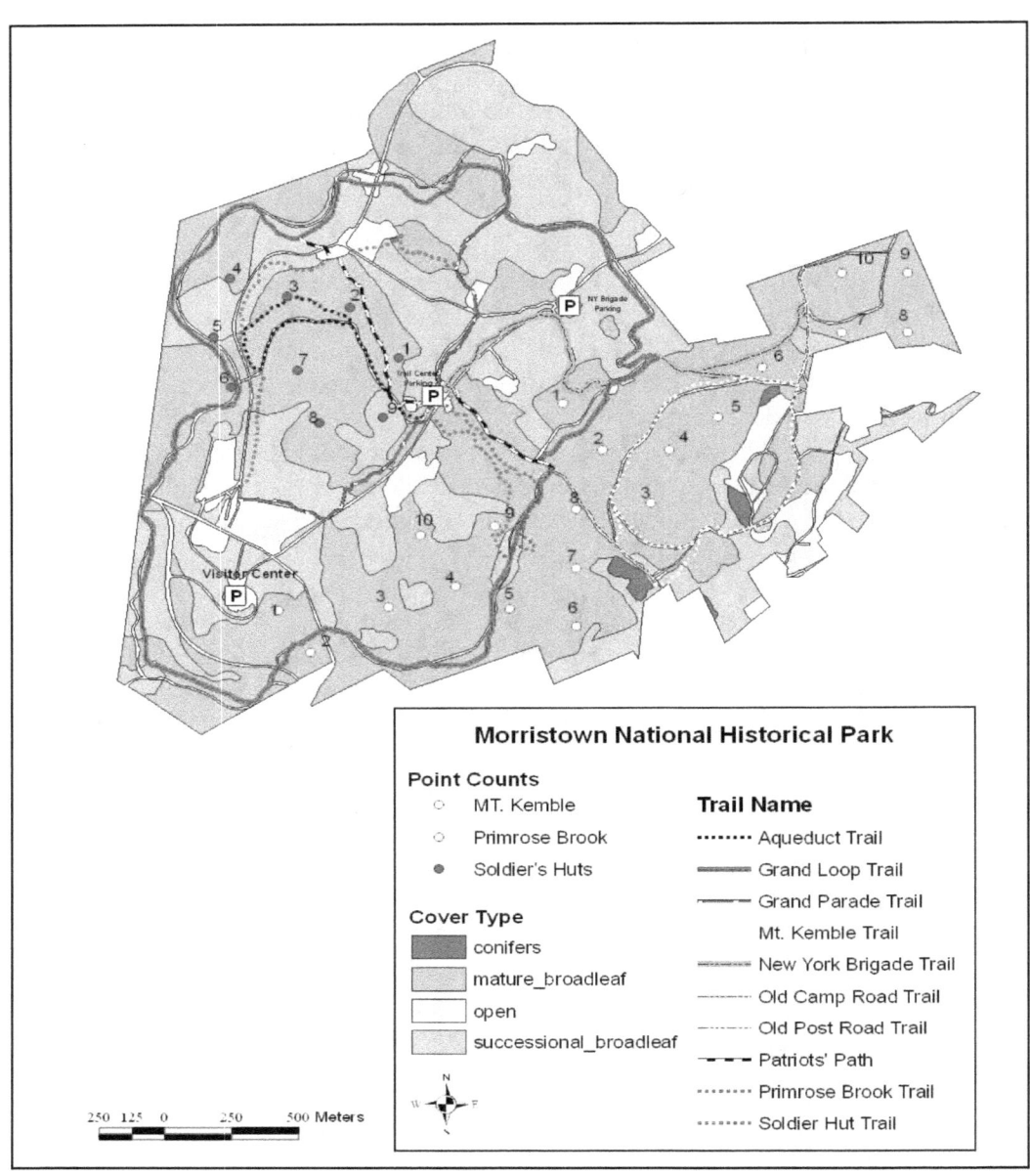

Figure 13. Breeding landbird monitoring point count locations at Morristown National Historical Park.

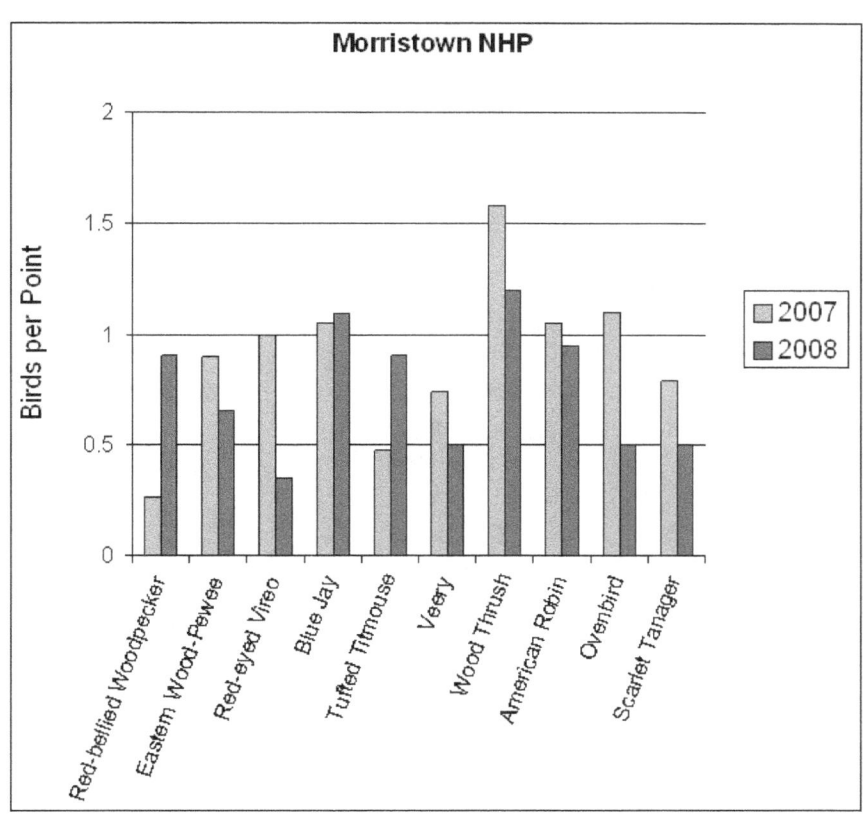

Figure 14. Relative abundance of the 10 most common species detected at Morristown National Historical Park in 2007 and 2008.

Table 8. Index of Biotic Integrity for Morristown National Historical Park for 2007 and 2008. Ranks that changed between years are in boldface.

Response Guild		Percent Species Richness		Biotic Integrity Rating	
		2007	2008	2007	2008
Composition:	Exotic	0%	0%	Good	Good
	Nest Pred / Brood Parasite	8%	6%	Good	Good
Resident		**28%**	**33%**	**Good**	**Caution**
	Single Brooded	47%	39%	Sig Conc	Sig Conc
Function:	Bark Prober	11%	14%	Good	Good
Ground	**Gleaner**	**11%**	**8%**	**Good**	**Caution**
	High Canopy Forager	8%	8%	Caution	Caution
	Low Canopy Forager	14%	11%	Sig Conc	Sig Conc
	Omnivore	33%	39%	Caution	Caution
Structure:	Canopy Nester	25%	22%	Caution	Caution
	Forest-ground Nester	17%	11%	Caution	Caution
	Interior Forest Obligate	28%	19%	Caution	Caution
	Shrub Nester	**22%**	**25%**	**Caution**	**Sig Conc**

Saint-Gaudens National Historic Site (New Hampshire)

Eight point counts (Figure 15) were established at Saint-Gaudens National Historic Site (SAGA), and surveyed in 2007 and 2008. The park was surveyed twice in 2008.

A total of 80 birds were detected in 2007, and 181 birds were detected in 2008 (including the repeat site visit). In total, 44 species were recorded, including several species that were only detected during the second survey in 2008 (Solitary Sandpiper, Great Crested Flycatcher, Yellow-throated Vireo, White-Breasted Nuthatch, and Yellow-rumped Warbler). There was an average abundance of 11.1 birds per point (excluding the second survey). In 2008, both relative abundance and species richness increased from the previous year. Three species of regional conservation concern were detected during the surveys: Belted Kingfisher, Willow Flycatcher, and Wood Thrush. A list of species, their relative abundances, and other summary statistics from the first survey of each point are provided in Appendix A. The most commonly detected species were Ovenbird and Red-eyed Vireo (Figure 16).

The park-wide IBI rating changed for three guilds between 2007 and 2008 (Table 9). "Significant Concern" ratings were rare, and composition metrics were generally "Good." The potential causes of the overall "Caution" ratings for structure and function might warrant further exploration, although this ranking may be partially due to incomplete characterization of the park's avian community.

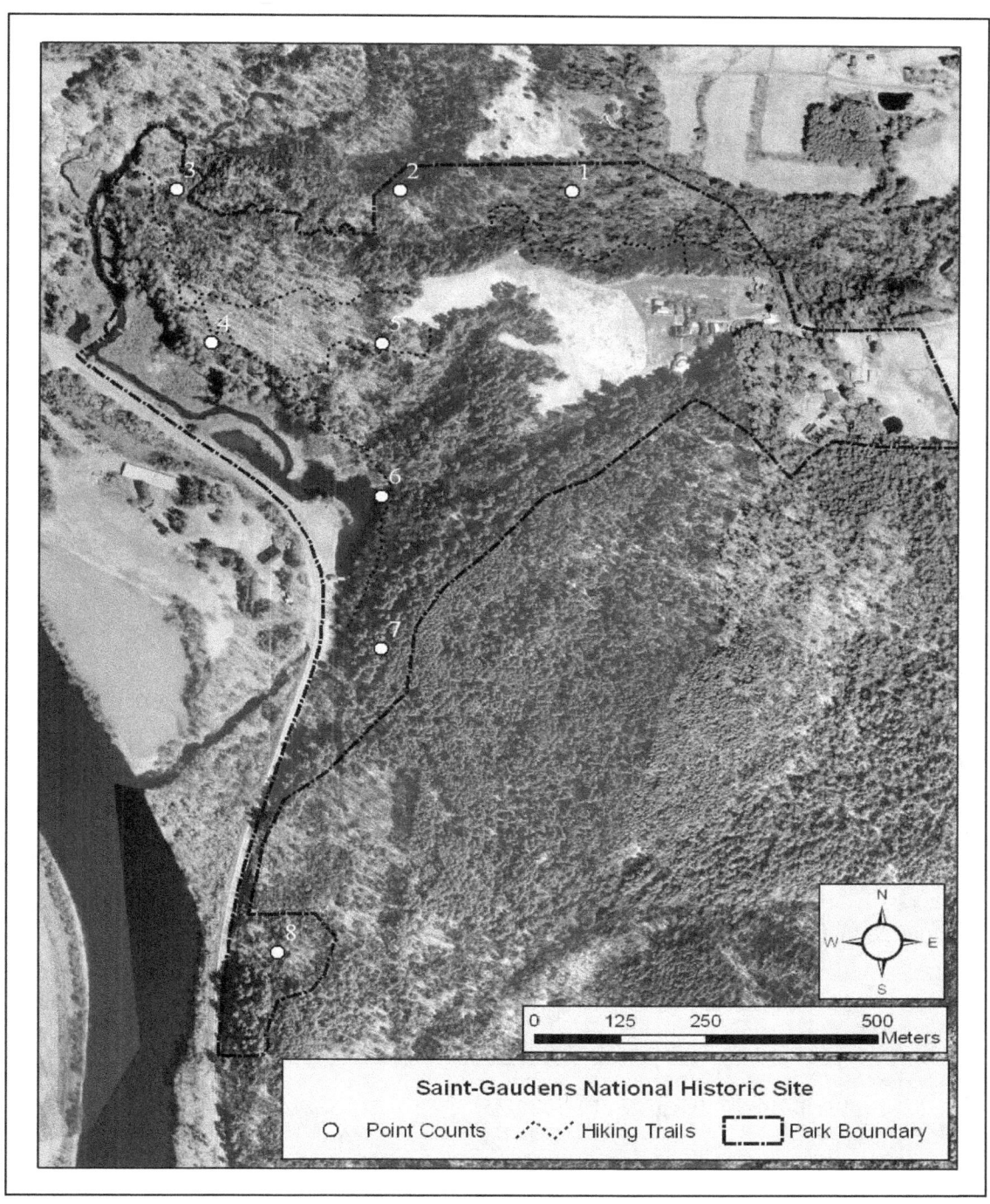

Figure 15. Breeding landbird monitoring point count locations at Saint-Gaudens National Historic Site.

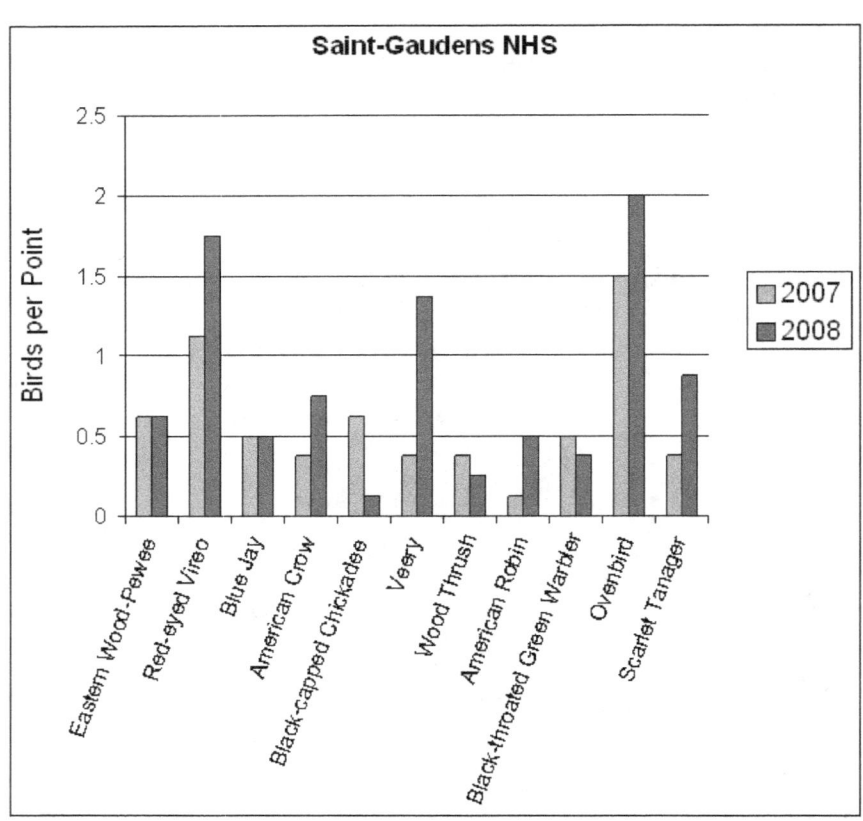

Figure 16. Relative abundance of the 10 most common species detected at Saint-Gaudens National Historic Site in 2007 and 2008.

Table 9. Index of Biotic Integrity for Saint-Gaudens National Historic Site for 2007 and 2008. Ranks that changed between years are in boldface.

		Percent Species Richness		Biotic Integrity Rating	
Response Guild		2007	2008	2007	2008
Composition:	Exotic	0%	0%	Good	Good
	Nest Pred / Brood Parasite	**11%**	**5%**	**Caution**	**Good**
	Resident	18%	16%	Good	Good
	Single Brooded	61%	55%	Caution	Caution
Function:	Bark Prober	11%	11%	Caution	Caution
	Ground Gleaner	**4%**	**8%**	**Sig Conc**	**Caution**
	High Canopy Forager	11%	11%	Caution	Caution
	Low Canopy Forager	21%	16%	Caution	Caution
	Omnivore	36%	34%	Caution	Caution
Structure:	Canopy Nester	32%	29%	Caution	Caution
	Forest-ground Nester	14%	16%	Caution	Caution
	Interior Forest Obligate	**36%**	**29%**	**Good**	**Caution**
	Shrub Nester	32%	26%	Sig Conc	Sig Conc

Saugus Iron Works National Historic Site (Massachusetts)

Three point counts were established in 2008 at Saugus Iron Works National Historic Site (SAIR) (Figure 17). A single survey of these three point counts was conducted by a volunteer observer during June 2008. In the future, efforts will be made to conduct multiple visits to the established survey points to increase sample size.

A total of 35 individual birds of 21 species were recorded, with a mean abundance of 11.7 birds per point. One species of conservation concern (Baltimore Oriole) and three non-native species (Rock Dove, European Starling, and House Sparrow) were detected. Appendix A contains a list of the species detected, relative abundance, and other summary statistics. American Crow, Song Sparrow, Northern Cardinal, and House Sparrow were the most commonly detected species (Figure 18).

Saugus Iron Works National Historic Site had park-wide IBI ratings of "Caution" and "Significant Concern." This is not surprising considering the heavily urbanized location of this small park (Table 10).

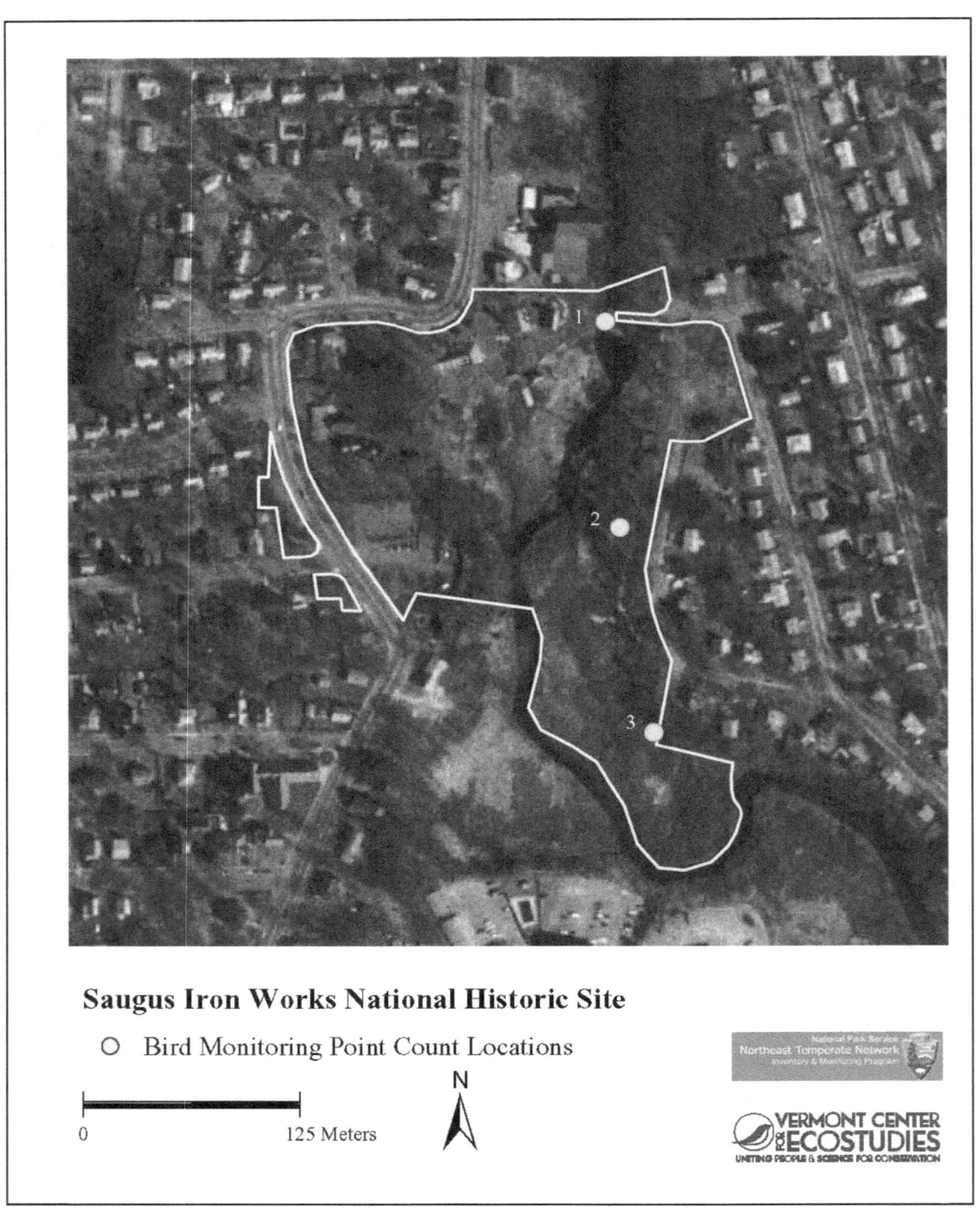

Saugus Iron Works National Historic Site

○ Bird Monitoring Point Count Locations

N

0   125 Meters

Figure 17. Breeding landbird monitoring point count locations at Saugus Iron Works Historic Site.

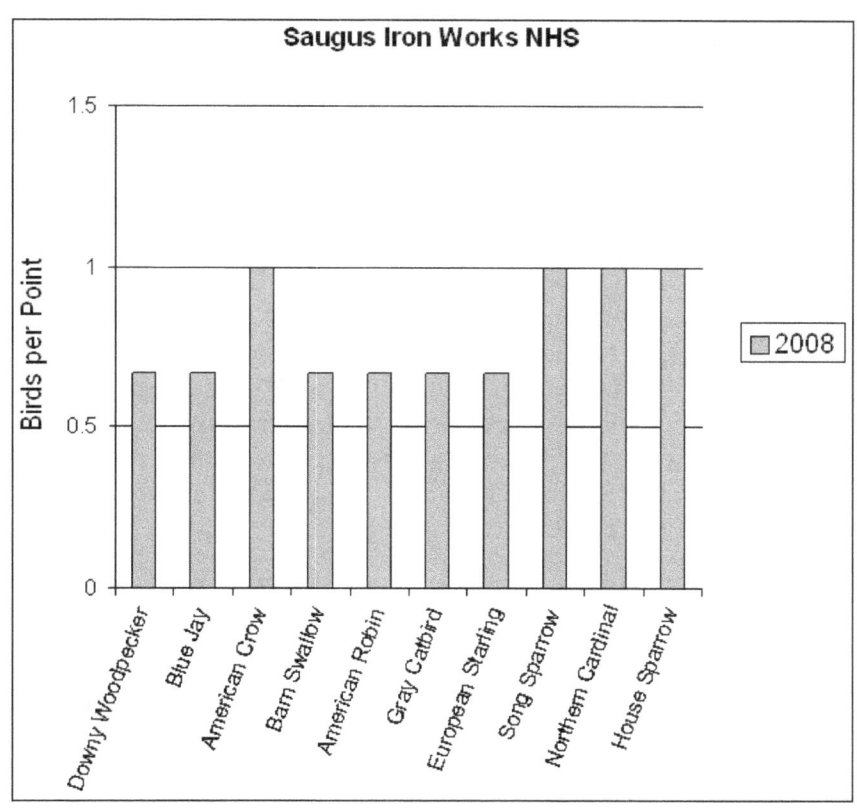

Figure 18. Relative abundance of the 10 most common species detected at Saugus Iron Works National Historic Site in 2008

Table 10. Index of Biotic Integrity for Saugus Iron Works National Historic Site for 2008.

Response Guild		Percent Species Richness 2008	Biotic Integrity Rating 2008
Composition:	Exotic	14%	Significant Concern
	Nest Pred / Brood Parasite	14%	Caution
	Resident	38%	Caution
	Single Brooded	14%	Significant Concern
Function:	Bark Prober	5%	Caution
	Ground Gleaner	5%	Caution
	High Canopy Forager	0%	Significant Concern
	Low Canopy Forager	5%	Significant Concern
	Omnivore	52%	Significant Concern
Structure:	Canopy Nester	19%	Caution
	Forest-ground Nester	0%	Significant Concern
	Interior Forest Obligate	0%	Significant Concern
	Shrub Nester	24%	Caution

Saratoga National Historical Park (New York)

A total of six study sites consisting of 51 point counts were established in 2006 and 2007 at the Saratoga National Historical Park (SARA). Three of these sites (25 points) are in grassland habitat, and three (26 points) are in forested habitat (Figure 19). Point count surveys were initiated in 2006 when four study sites were sampled (three grassland, one forest). In 2007, two sites (Middle Ravine and Freeman Farm Grassland) were surveyed, and in 2008 all sites were sampled.

A total of 318 birds were detected in 2007, and 830 birds were detected in 2008. In total, 68 species were recorded, and there was an average abundance of 16.1 birds per point. Eight species of conservation concern were detected during the surveys: Black-Billed Cuckoo, Eastern Wood-Pewee, Wood Thrush, Blue-winged Warbler, Golden-winged Warbler, Eastern Towhee, Field Sparrow, and Baltimore Oriole. A list of species, their relative abundances, and other summary statistics are provided in Appendices A and B. Red-winged Blackbird, Goldfinch, and Ovenbird were the most commonly detected species (Figure 20).

The forest IBI for Saratoga National Historical Park results showed a change in rating for four guilds between 2007 and 2008. While compositional metrics generally were rated "Good," structural and functional metrics received a "Caution" or "Significant Concern" rating. The forest bird community may be affected by the generally fragmented landscape around the park (Table 11). The forest IBI has also been calculated for each forest site, and these results are in Appendix C.

The grassland assessment had three "Caution" metric ratings and one "Good" metric rating; this community is known to be at risk in the region, and it would be prudent for the park to continue its efforts to manage grassland habitat to support avian diversity (Table 12).

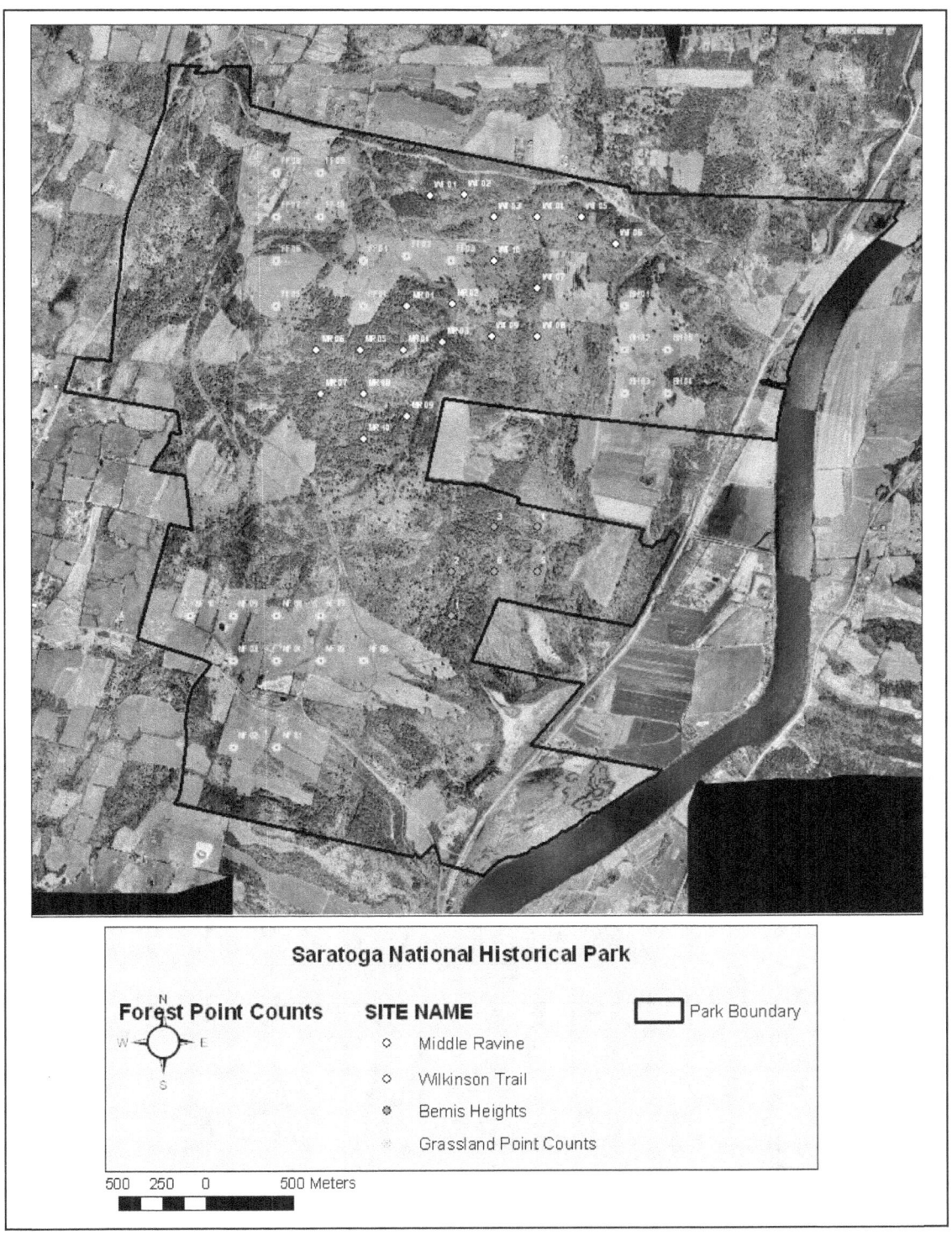

Figure 19. Breeding landbird monitoring point count locations at Saratoga National Historical Park.

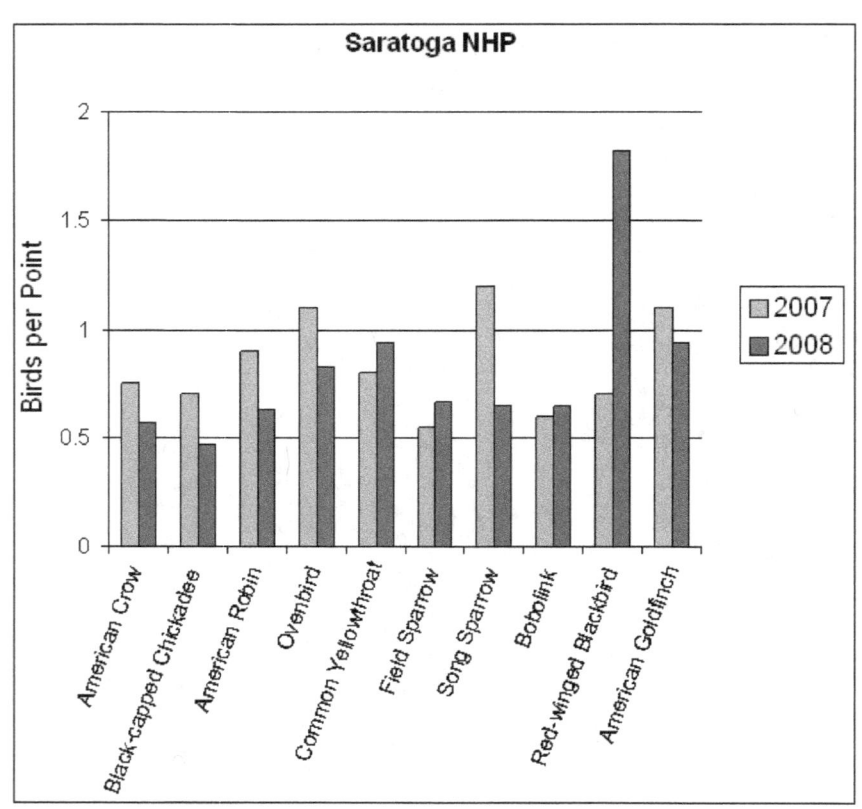

Figure 20. Relative abundance of the 10 most common species detected at Saratoga National Historical Park in 2007 and 2008.

Table 11. Forest Index of Biotic Integrity for Saratoga National Historical Park for 2007 and 2008. Ranks that changed between years are in boldface.

		Percent Species Richness		Biotic Integrity Rating	
Response Guild		2007	2008	2007	2008
Composition:	Exotic	0%	0%	Good	Good
	Nest Pred / Brood Parasite	8%	6%	Good	Good
	Resident	28%	26%	Good	Good
Single	**Brooded**	**50%**	**49% Caution**		**Sig Conc**
Function:	**Bark Prober**	**8% 13%**		**Caution**	**Good**
Grou	**nd Gleaner**	**11%**	**4%**	**Good**	**Caution**
	High Canopy Forager	6%	6%	Sig Conc	Sig Conc
	Low Canopy Forager	**14%**	**15%**	**Sig Conc**	**Caution**
	Omnivore	44%	36%	Caution	Caution
Structure:	Canopy Nester	25%	23%	Caution	Caution
	Forest-ground Nester	11%	15%	Caution	Caution
	Interior Forest Obligate	22%	26%	Caution	Caution
	Shrub Nester	25%	30%	Sig Conc	Sig Conc

34

Table 12. Grassland assessment for Saratoga National Historical Park for 2007 and 2008.

	Percent Species Richness		Biotic Integrity Rating	
Response Guild	2007	2008	2007	2008
Edge Generalist	28%	30%	Caution	Caution
Exotic	0%	0%	Good	Good
Grassland Obligate	6%	9%	Caution	Caution
Shrub-dependent	19%	17%	Caution	Caution

Vanderbilt Mansion National Historic Site (New York)

The Roosevelt-Vanderbilt National Historic Sites (ROVA) consist of three separate park units at which study sites were established and surveyed in 2006, 2007, and 2008. Seven point counts were established at the Vanderbilt Mansion National Historic Site (VAMA) (Figure 21).

Sixty-three individual birds were detected in 2007, and 43 birds were detected in 2008. In total, 25 species were recorded, and there was an average abundance of 7.6 birds per point. In 2008, relative abundance declined but species richness increased. Two species of conservation concern, Wood Thrush and Worm-eating Warbler, were detected during the past two survey years. A list of species, their relative abundances, and other summary statistics are provided in Appendix A. Red-eyed Vireo, Wood Thrush, and Northern Cardinal were the most commonly detected species (Figure 22).

The park-wide IBI rating changed for several guilds between 2007 and 2008. The park received an average rating of "Caution," perhaps indicative of its location on a fragmented landscape, although the IBI may also have been affected by the low number of counts, which probably reduced the number of species detected (Table 13).

Figure 21. Breeding landbird monitoring point count locations at Vanderbilt Mansion National Historic Site.

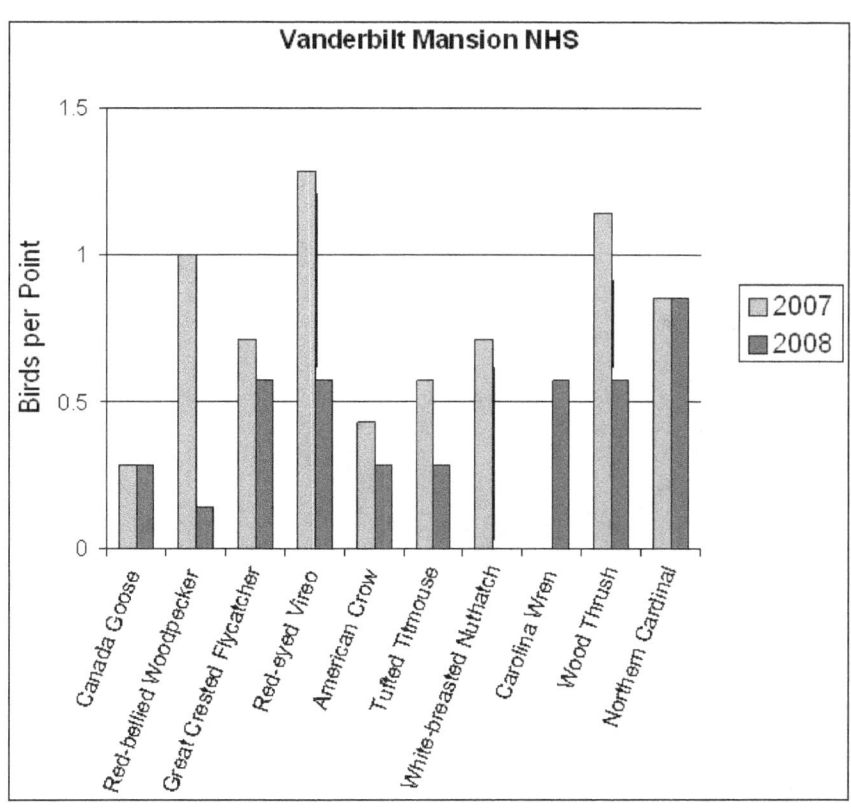

Figure 22. Relative abundance of the 10 most common species detected at Vanderbilt Mansion National Historic Site in 2007 and 2008.

Table 13. Index of Biotic Integrity for Vanderbilt Mansion National Historical Site for 2007 and 2008. Ranks that changed between years are in boldface.

Response Guild		Percent Species Richness		Biotic Integrity Rating	
		2007	2008	2007	2008
Composition:	Exotic	0%	0%	Good	Good
	Nest Pred / Brood Parasite	**11%**	**5%**	**Caution**	**Good**
	Resident	39%	35%	Caution	Caution
	Single Brooded	39%	30%	Sig Conc	Sig Conc
Function:	Bark Prober	22%	15%	Good	Good
	Ground Gleaner	17%	10%	Good	Good
	High Canopy Forager	**6%**	**10%**	**Sig Conc**	**Caution**
	Low Canopy Forager	11%	10%	Sig Conc	Sig Conc
Om	**nivore**	**28%**	**30%**	**Good**	**Caution**
Structure:	Canopy Nester	17%	15%	Caution	Caution
	Forest-ground Nester	11%	10%	Caution	Caution
	Interior Forest Obligate	28%	20%	Caution	Caution
	Shrub Nester	**22%**	**30%**	**Caution**	**Sig Conc**

Weir Farm National Historic Site (Connecticut)

Five point count stations were established at Weir Farm National Historic Site in 2006 (Figure 23). A volunteer conducted surveys in June 2006, but was unable to continue in 2007. A new observer was recruited and conducted point count surveys in 2008, however, to date, survey data have not been submitted, despite repeated requests.

Figure 23. Breeding landbird monitoring point count locations at Weir Farm National Historic Site.

Literature Cited

Browder, S. F., D. H. Johnson, and I. J. Ball. 2002. Assemblages of breeding birds as indicators of grassland condition. Ecological Indicators **2**:257-270.

Coppedge, B. R., D. M. Engle, R.E. Masters, and M. S. Gregory. 2006. Development of a grassland integrity index based on breeding bird assemblages. Environmental Monitoring and Assessment **118**:125-145.

Faccio, S. D., B. R. Mitchell, and P. Pooler. 2009. Draft Landbird Vital Sign Monitoring Protocol. http://science.nature.nps.gov/im/units/NETN/monitor/birds/birds.cfm.

Glennon, M. J. and W. F. Porter. 2005. Effects of land use management on biotic integrity: An investigation of bird communities. Biological Conservation **126**:499-511.

North American Bird Conservation Initiative. 2000. North American Bird Conservation Initiative: Bird conservation region descriptions. U.S. Fish and Wildlife Service, Washington DC.

O'Connell, T. J., L. E. Jackson and R. P. Brooks. 2000. Bird guilds as indicators of ecological condition in the central Appalachians. Ecological Application **10**:1706-1721.

Appendix A. Summary of species detected during monitoring activities in Northeast Temperate Network parks.

This appendix contains a list of species detected during monitoring activities in each park, and the relative abundance (birds per point) of each species for each year. It only includes data for the first survey of each point in a given year, in order to promote more consistent comparisons between years and to avoid artificially inflating abundances due to counting the same individuals in repeat visits. Species in boldface are species of regional or continental concern, and species in italics are the 10 most common species for each park. There will occasionally be more than 10 italicized species, if multiple species have the same abundance.

This appendix also lists the number of points surveyed per park each year, the number of birds detected per point count, the species richness, and the Shannon diversity index for each park for each year.

Appendix A. Summary of species detected during monitoring activities in Northeast Temperate Network parks (continued).

Acadia National Park

Common Name	2007	2008	Mean
Common Loon	0.00	0.04	0.02
Herring Gull	0.04	0.00	0.02
Mourning Dove	*0.64*	*0.61*	*0.63*
Hairy Woodpecker	0.21	0.00	0.11
Pileated Woodpecker	0.18	0.09	0.13
Alder Flycatcher	0.04	0.00	0.02
Least Flycatcher	0.14	0.09	0.11
Great Crested Flycatcher	0.04	0.00	0.02
Blue-headed Vireo	*0.36*	*0.61*	*0.48*
Red-eyed Vireo	0.00	0.04	0.02
Blue Jay	0.18	0.17	0.18
American Crow	*0.39*	*0.48*	*0.44*
Common Raven	0.32	0.09	0.20
Black-capped Chickadee	0.14	0.35	0.25
Boreal Chickadee	**0.21**	**0.00**	**0.11**
Red-breasted Nuthatch	*0.50*	*0.26*	*0.38*
Brown Creeper	0.07	0.35	0.21
Winter Wren	0.25	0.22	0.23
Golden-crowned Kinglet	*0.36*	*0.83*	*0.59*
Ruby-crowned Kinglet	0.07	0.00	0.04
Swainson's Thrush	0.14	0.04	0.09
Hermit Thrush	0.36	0.04	0.20
Wood Thrush	**0.04**	**0.00**	**0.02**
American Robin	*0.46*	*0.30*	*0.38*
Brown Thrasher	0.04	0.00	0.02
Cedar Waxwing	0.11	0.04	0.08
Northern Parula	0.04	0.00	0.02
Chestnut-sided Warbler	0.07	0.00	0.04
Magnolia Warbler	0.14	0.17	0.16
Black-throated Blue Warbler	0.07	0.30	0.19
Yellow-rumped Warbler (Myrtle Warbler)	0.11	0.30	0.21
Black-throated Green Warbler	*1.75*	*1.87*	*1.81*
Blackburnian Warbler	*0.29*	*0.39*	*0.34*
Blackpoll Warbler	**0.00**	**0.04**	**0.02**
Black-and-white Warbler	0.14	0.04	0.09
Ovenbird	*0.68*	*1.43*	*1.06*
Common Yellowthroat	0.00	0.04	0.02
Eastern Towhee	**0.04**	**0.00**	**0.02**
Dark-eyed Junco (Slate-colored Junco)	0.21	0.17	0.19
Red-winged Blackbird	0.04	0.09	0.06
Common Grackle	0.04	0.00	0.02
Purple Finch	0.18	0.13	0.15
Pine Siskin	*0.29*	*0.65*	*0.47*
Points Surveyed:	28	23	
Birds per Point:	9.36	10.30	9.83
Species Richness:	39	31	43
Shannon Diversity:	3.173	2.885	

Eleanor Roosevelt National Historic Site

Common Name	2007	2008	Mean
Cooper's Hawk	0.09	0.00	0.05
Mourning Dove	0.27	0.00	0.14
Barred Owl	0.09	0.00	0.05
Ruby-throated Hummingbird	0.00	0.09	0.05
Red-bellied Woodpecker	*0.55*	*0.36*	*0.45*
Downy Woodpecker	0.00	0.18	0.09
Hairy Woodpecker	0.18	0.36	0.27
Northern Flicker (Yellow-shafted Flicker)	0.00	0.18	0.09
Pileated Woodpecker	0.09	0.27	0.18
Eastern Wood-Pewee	**0.27**	**0.09**	**0.18**
Great Crested Flycatcher	0.09	0.09	0.09
Red-eyed Vireo	*0.91*	*0.64*	*0.77*
Blue Jay	0.27	0.27	0.27
American Crow	*0.45*	*0.36*	*0.41*
Black-capped Chickadee	0.00	0.09	0.05
Tufted Titmouse	*1.27*	*0.27*	*0.77*
White-breasted Nuthatch	*0.45*	*0.82*	*0.64*
Brown Creeper	0.09	0.00	0.05
Veery	0.27	0.27	0.27
Wood Thrush	***1.27***	***0.55***	***0.91***
American Robin	*0.73*	*0.73*	*0.73*
Gray Catbird	*0.36*	*0.36*	*0.36*
Worm-eating Warbler	**0.09**	**0.00**	**0.05**
Ovenbird	*0.36*	*0.45*	*0.41*
Scarlet Tanager	0.09	0.36	0.23
Song Sparrow	0.09	0.00	0.05
Northern Cardinal	*1.09*	*0.45*	*0.77*
Rose-breasted Grosbeak	0.36	0.00	0.18
Red-winged Blackbird	0.18	0.00	0.09
Common Grackle	0.09	0.00	0.05
Baltimore Oriole	**0.09**	**0.09**	**0.09**
American Goldfinch	0.09	0.09	0.09
Points Surveyed:	11	11	
Birds per Point:	10.27	7.45	8.86
Species Richness:	28	23	32
Shannon Diversity:	2.933	2.936	

Appendix A. Summary of species detected during monitoring activities in Northeast Temperate Network parks (continued).

Home of Franklin D. Roosevelt National Historical Site

Common Name	2007	2008	Mean
Canada Goose	0.08	0.00	0.04
Mute Swan	0.00	0.08	0.04
Wild Turkey	0.08	0.00	0.04
Red-tailed Hawk	0.08	0.00	0.04
Mourning Dove	*0.33*	*0.50*	*0.42*
Yellow-billed Cuckoo	0.08	0.00	0.04
Red-bellied Woodpecker	*0.58*	*0.50*	*0.54*
Downy Woodpecker	0.17	0.17	0.17
Northern Flicker (Yellow-shafted Flicker)	0.00	0.25	0.13
Pileated Woodpecker	0.25	0.08	0.17
Eastern Wood-Pewee	**0.17**	**0.17**	**0.17**
Least Flycatcher	0.08	0.00	0.04
Great Crested Flycatcher	0.33	0.00	0.17
Yellow-throated Vireo	0.00	0.08	0.04
Blue-headed Vireo	0.08	0.00	0.04
Red-eyed Vireo	*0.67*	*0.58*	*0.63*
Blue Jay	*0.42*	*0.42*	*0.42*
American Crow	0.00	0.25	0.13
Fish Crow	0.08	0.08	0.08
Black-capped Chickadee	0.33	0.17	0.25
Tufted Titmouse	*1.08*	*0.92*	*1.00*
White-breasted Nuthatch	*0.33*	*0.50*	*0.42*
Brown Creeper	0.00	0.08	0.04
Carolina Wren	0.00	0.17	0.08
Blue-gray Gnatcatcher	0.08	0.00	0.04
Wood Thrush	***0.58***	***0.58***	***0.58***
American Robin	*0.67*	*0.42*	*0.54*
Ovenbird	0.00	0.08	0.04
Louisiana Waterthrush	0.25	0.08	0.17
Scarlet Tanager	*0.50*	*0.42*	*0.46*
Northern Cardinal	*0.25*	*0.33*	*0.29*
Rose-breasted Grosbeak	0.17	0.00	0.08
Red-winged Blackbird	0.25	0.00	0.13
Brown-headed Cowbird	0.17	0.00	0.08
Baltimore Oriole	**0.17**	**0.00**	**0.08**
American Goldfinch	0.08	0.00	0.04
Points Surveyed:	12	12	
Birds per Point:	8.42	6.92	7.67
Species Richness:	29	23	36
Shannon Diversity:	3.081	2.880	

Appendix A. Summary of species detected during monitoring activities in Northeast Temperate Network parks (continued).

Marsh-Billings-Rockefeller National Historical Park

Common Name	2007	2008	Mean
Wild Turkey	0.00	0.05	0.03
Mourning Dove	0.16	0.15	0.16
Barred Owl	0.28	0.00	0.14
Yellow-bellied Sapsucker	0.32	0.20	0.26
Downy Woodpecker	0.12	0.00	0.06
Hairy Woodpecker	0.20	0.20	0.20
Northern Flicker (Yellow-shafted Flicker)	0.04	0.00	0.02
Pileated Woodpecker	0.04	0.00	0.02
Eastern Wood-Pewee	*0.72*	*0.55*	*0.64*
Least Flycatcher	0.12	0.05	0.09
Great Crested Flycatcher	0.04	0.25	0.15
Eastern Kingbird	0.04	0.00	0.02
Blue-headed Vireo	0.20	0.20	0.20
Red-eyed Vireo	*1.80*	*1.85*	*1.83*
Blue Jay	*0.84*	*0.40*	*0.62*
American Crow	0.36	0.15	0.26
Common Raven	0.00	0.05	0.03
Black-capped Chickadee	*0.84*	*0.50*	*0.67*
Tufted Titmouse	0.04	0.05	0.05
Red-breasted Nuthatch	0.08	0.00	0.04
White-breasted Nuthatch	0.32	0.10	0.21
Brown Creeper	*0.56*	*0.40*	*0.48*
Winter Wren	0.04	0.20	0.12
Golden-crowned Kinglet	0.04	0.05	0.05
Veery	0.12	0.10	0.11
Hermit Thrush	*0.72*	*1.05*	*0.89*
Wood Thrush	**0.24**	**0.35**	**0.30**
American Robin	*0.64*	*0.35*	*0.50*
Cedar Waxwing	0.04	0.05	0.05
Chestnut-sided Warbler	0.00	0.05	0.03
Black-throated Blue Warbler	0.24	0.15	0.20
Yellow-rumped Warbler (Myrtle Warbler)	0.08	0.05	0.07
Black-throated Green Warbler	*0.72*	*0.60*	*0.66*
Blackburnian Warbler	*0.68*	*0.50*	*0.59*
Pine Warbler	0.04	0.10	0.07
Black-and-white Warbler	0.08	0.00	0.04
American Redstart	0.04	0.00	0.02
Ovenbird	*3.36*	*3.45*	*3.41*
Louisiana Waterthrush	0.08	0.00	0.04
Common Yellowthroat	0.12	0.20	0.16
Scarlet Tanager	0.56	0.25	0.41
Chipping Sparrow	0.04	0.00	0.02
Dark-eyed Junco (Slate-colored Junco)	0.44	0.05	0.25
Rose-breasted Grosbeak	0.12	0.05	0.09
Indigo Bunting	0.20	0.10	0.15
Bobolink	**0.04**	**0.00**	**0.02**
Red-winged Blackbird	0.28	0.15	0.22

Appendix A. Summary of species detected during monitoring activities in Northeast Temperate Network parks (continued).

Common Name	2007	2008	Mean
Common Grackle	0.04	0.00	0.02
Brown-headed Cowbird	0.08	0.05	0.07
Purple Finch	0.04	0.00	0.02
American Goldfinch	0.04	0.05	0.05
Points Surveyed:	25	20	
Birds per Point:	16.28	13.10	14.69
Species Richness:	48	38	51
Shannon Diversity:	3.122	2.839	

Minute Man National Historical Park

Common Name	2007	2008	Mean
Canada Goose	0.04	0.00	0.02
Mourning Dove	0.00	0.09	0.04
Black-billed Cuckoo	**0.00**	**0.04**	**0.02**
Chimney Swift	**0.09**	**0.00**	**0.04**
Red-bellied Woodpecker	0.09	0.13	0.11
Downy Woodpecker	*0.52*	*0.30*	*0.41*
Hairy Woodpecker	0.17	0.00	0.09
Northern Flicker (Yellow-shafted Flicker)	0.00	0.13	0.07
Eastern Wood-Pewee	**0.26**	**0.13**	**0.20**
Eastern Phoebe	0.00	0.04	0.02
Great Crested Flycatcher	0.00	0.22	0.11
Warbling Vireo	0.00	0.04	0.02
Red-eyed Vireo	0.09	0.35	0.22
Blue Jay	*1.13*	*1.22*	*1.17*
American Crow	*0.74*	*0.83*	*0.78*
Black-capped Chickadee	*0.65*	*0.48*	*0.57*
Tufted Titmouse	*1.48*	*1.43*	*1.46*
White-breasted Nuthatch	0.39	0.13	0.26
Carolina Wren	0.17	0.00	0.09
House Wren	0.04	0.00	0.02
Veery	**0.13**	**0.00**	**0.07**
Wood Thrush	**0.30**	**0.35**	**0.33**
American Robin	*0.91*	*1.13*	*1.02*
Gray Catbird	*0.48*	*0.48*	*0.48*
Northern Mockingbird	0.09	0.00	0.04
Cedar Waxwing	0.04	0.00	0.02
Yellow Warbler	0.00	0.13	0.07
Pine Warbler	0.30	0.39	0.35
American Redstart	0.04	0.00	0.02
Ovenbird	*0.52*	*0.30*	*0.41*
Common Yellowthroat	0.43	0.35	0.39
Scarlet Tanager	**0.09**	**0.22**	**0.15**
Chipping Sparrow	0.00	0.17	0.09
Song Sparrow	*0.61*	*0.48*	*0.54*
Swamp Sparrow	0.00	0.04	0.02
Northern Cardinal	*0.74*	*0.70*	*0.72*

Appendix A. Summary of species detected during monitoring activities in Northeast Temperate Network parks (continued).

Common Name	2007	2008	Mean
Rose-breasted Grosbeak	**0.17**	**0.13**	**0.15**
Indigo Bunting	0.13	0.13	0.13
Red-winged Blackbird	*0.43*	*0.48*	*0.46*
Common Grackle	0.13	0.09	0.11
Brown-headed Cowbird	0.48	0.13	0.30
Balt imore Oriole	**0.13**	**0.00**	**0.07**
House Finch	0.09	0.04	0.07
American Goldfinch	0.48	0.22	0.35
House Sparrow	0.13	0.04	0.09
Points Surveyed:	23	23	
Birds per Point:	12.74	11.57	12.15
Species Richness:	36	35	45
Shannon Diversity:	3.201	3.121	

Morristown National Historical Park

Common Name	2007	2008	Mean
Wild Turkey	0.11	0.00	0.05
Red-tailed Hawk	0.05	0.10	0.08
Mourning Dove	0.05	0.15	0.10
Yellow-billed Cuckoo	0.21	0.05	0.13
Great Horned Owl	0.00	0.10	0.05
Red-bellied Woodpecker	*0.26*	*0.90*	*0.58*
Downy Woodpecker	0.11	0.30	0.20
Hairy Woodpecker	0.00	0.25	0.13
Northern Flicker (Yellow-shafted Flicker)	0.53	0.25	0.39
Pileated Woodpecker	0.11	0.10	0.10
Eastern Wood-Pewee	**0.89**	**0.65**	**0.77**
Eastern Phoebe	0.05	0.05	0.05
Great Crested Flycatcher	0.05	0.20	0.13
Yellow-throated Vireo	**0.11**	**0.05**	**0.08**
Red-eyed Vireo	*1.00*	*0.35*	*0.68*
Blue Jay	*1.05*	*1.10*	*1.08*
American Crow	0.47	0.40	0.44
Black-capped Chickadee	0.05	0.05	0.05
Tufted Titmouse	*0.47*	*0.90*	*0.69*
White-breasted Nuthatch	0.26	0.60	0.43
Carolina Wren	0.11	0.00	0.05
House Wren	0.00	0.05	0.03
Eastern Bluebird	0.00	0.15	0.08
Veery	*0.74*	*0.50*	*0.62*
Wood Thrush	***1.58***	***1.20***	***1.39***
American Robin	*1.05*	*0.95*	*1.00*
Gray Catbird	0.11	0.10	0.10
American Redstart	0.32	0.00	0.16
Worm-eating Warbler	**0.21**	**0.20**	**0.21**
Ovenbird	*1.11*	*0.50*	*0.80*
Louisiana Waterthrush	**0.11**	**0.00**	**0.05**

Appendix A. Summary of species detected during monitoring activities in Northeast Temperate Network parks (continued).

Common Name	2007	2008	Mean
Kentucky Warbler	**0.05**	**0.00**	**0.03**
Hooded Warbler	0.21	0.00	0.11
Scarlet Tanager	*0.79*	*0.50*	*0.64*
Eastern Towhee	**0.53**	**0.05**	**0.29**
Chipping Sparrow	0.05	0.00	0.03
Northern Cardinal	0.47	0.10	0.29
Rose-breasted Grosbeak	0.21	0.10	0.16
Indigo Bunting	0.00	0.10	0.05
Brown-headed Cowbird	0.16	0.00	0.08
Baltimore Oriole	0.11	0.30	0.20
Points Surveyed:	19	20	
Birds per Point:	13.74	11.35	12.54
Species Richness:	36	33	41
Shannon Diversity:	3.127	3.082	

Saint-Gaudens National Historic Site

Common Name	2007	2008	Mean
Belted Kingfisher	**0.00**	**0.13**	**0.06**
Yellow-bellied Sapsucker	0.25	0.00	0.13
Hairy Woodpecker	0.13	0.00	0.06
Northern Flicker (Yellow-shafted Flicker)	0.00	0.13	0.06
Pileated Woodpecker	0.38	0.00	0.19
Eastern Wood-Pewee	*0.63*	*0.63*	*0.63*
Willow Flycatcher	**0.13**	**0.00**	**0.06**
Least Flycatcher	0.13	0.25	0.19
Eastern Phoebe	0.00	0.13	0.06
Blue-headed Vireo	0.13	0.00	0.06
"Solitary" Vireo (Solitary Vireo complex)	0.00	0.13	0.06
Red-eyed Vireo	*1.13*	*1.75*	*1.44*
Blue Jay	*0.50*	*0.50*	*0.50*
American Crow	*0.38*	*0.75*	*0.56*
Black-capped Chickadee	*0.63*	*0.13*	*0.38*
Tufted Titmouse	0.13	0.00	0.06
Veery	*0.38*	*1.38*	*0.88*
Hermit Thrush	0.00	0.13	0.06
Wood Thrush	***0.38***	***0.25***	***0.31***
American Robin	*0.13*	*0.50*	*0.31*
Gray Catbird	0.25	0.13	0.19
Yellow Warbler	0.13	0.00	0.06
Chestnut-sided Warbler	0.25	0.13	0.19
Magnolia Warbler	0.00	0.13	0.06
Black-throated Green Warbler	*0.50*	*0.38*	*0.44*
Pine Warbler	0.00	0.25	0.13
Black-and-white Warbler	0.25	0.13	0.19
American Redstart	0.25	0.00	0.13
Ovenbird	*1.50*	*2.00*	*1.75*
Louisiana Waterthrush	0.25	0.13	0.19

Common Name	2007	2008	Mean
Common Yellowthroat	0.25	0.25	0.25
Scarlet Tanager	*0.38*	*0.88*	*0.63*
Song Sparrow	0.00	0.13	0.06
White-throated Sparrow	0.00	0.13	0.06
Rose-breasted Grosbeak	0.00	0.13	0.06
Red-winged Blackbird	0.25	0.25	0.25
Brown-headed Cowbird	0.25	0.00	0.13
Baltimore Oriole	0.13	0.13	0.13
American Goldfinch	0.00	0.25	0.13
Points Surveyed:	8	8	
Birds per Point:	10.00	12.13	11.06
Species Richness:	28	30	39
Shannon Diversity:	3.060	2.896	

Saugus Iron Works National Historic Site

Common Name	2007	2008	Mean
Mallard		0.33	0.33
Herring Gull		0.33	0.33
Rock Pigeon		0.33	0.33
Mourning Dove		0.33	0.33
Belted Kingfisher		0.33	0.33
Downy Woodpecker		*0.67*	*0.67*
Northern Flicker (Yellow-shafted Flicker)		0.33	0.33
Blue Jay		*0.67*	*0.67*
American Crow		*1.00*	*1.00*
Barn Swallow		*0.67*	*0.67*
Tufted Titmouse		0.33	0.33
American Robin		*0.67*	*0.67*
Gray Catbird		*0.67*	*0.67*
European Starling		*0.67*	*0.67*
Common Yellowthroat		0.33	0.33
Song Sparrow		*1.00*	*1.00*
Northern Cardinal		*1.00*	*1.00*
Red-winged Blackbird		0.33	0.33
Common Grackle		0.33	0.33
Baltimore Oriole		**0.33**	**0.33**
House Sparrow		*1.00*	*1.00*
Points Surveyed:		3	
Birds per Point:		11.67	11.67
Species Richness:		21	21
Shannon Diversity:		2.941	

Appendix A. Summary of species detected during monitoring activities in Northeast Temperate Network parks (continued).

Saratoga National Historical Park

Common Name	2007	2008	Mean
Canada Goose	0.05	0.08	0.06
Great Blue Heron	0.05	0.00	0.03
American Kestrel	0.00	0.04	0.02
Mourning Dove	0.55	0.43	0.49
Black-billed Cuckoo	**0.00**	**0.04**	**0.02**
Yellow-billed Cuckoo	0.00	0.02	0.01
Red-bellied Woodpecker	0.00	0.04	0.02
Yellow-bellied Sapsucker	0.05	0.14	0.09
Downy Woodpecker	0.10	0.20	0.15
Northern Flicker (Yellow-shafted Flicker)	0.15	0.04	0.09
Pileated Woodpecker	0.00	0.04	0.02
Eastern Wood-Pewee	**0.30**	**0.59**	**0.44**
Acadian Flycatcher	0.00	0.02	0.01
Alder Flycatcher	0.05	0.08	0.06
Willow Flycatcher	0.00	0.16	0.08
Least Flycatcher	0.00	0.08	0.04
Eastern Phoebe	0.05	0.08	0.06
Great Crested Flycatcher	0.55	0.35	0.45
Eastern Kingbird	0.10	0.16	0.13
Yellow-throated Vireo	0.05	0.02	0.03
Warbling Vireo	0.00	0.02	0.01
Red-eyed Vireo	0.50	0.49	0.50
Blue Jay	0.40	0.37	0.39
American Crow	*0.75*	*0.57*	*0.66*
Tree Swallow	0.40	0.20	0.30
Black-capped Chickadee	*0.70*	*0.47*	*0.59*
Tufted Titmouse	0.30	0.31	0.31
Red-breasted Nuthatch	0.00	0.04	0.02
White-breasted Nuthatch	0.15	0.06	0.10
Brown Creeper	0.05	0.14	0.09
House Wren	0.00	0.02	0.01
Winter Wren	0.05	0.00	0.03
Blue-gray Gnatcatcher	0.00	0.06	0.03
Eastern Bluebird	0.00	0.02	0.01
Veery	0.10	0.18	0.14
Hermit Thrush	0.05	0.10	0.07
Wood Thrush	**0.50**	**0.39**	**0.45**
American Robin	*0.90*	*0.63*	*0.76*
Gray Catbird	0.05	0.16	0.10
Cedar Waxwing	0.60	0.22	0.41
Blue-winged Warbler	**0.20**	**0.20**	**0.20**
G olden-winged Warbler	**0.10**	**0.00**	**0.05**
Yellow Warbler	0.10	0.16	0.13
Chestnut-sided Warbler	0.10	0.20	0.15
Yellow-rumped Warbler (Myrtle Warbler)	0.00	0.04	0.02
Prairie Warbler	0.15	0.06	0.10
Black-and-white Warbler	0.00	0.04	0.02

Appendix A. Summary of species detected during monitoring activities in Northeast Temperate Network parks (continued).

Common Name	2007	2008	Mean
American Redstart	0.05	0.00	0.03
Ovenbird	*1.10*	*0.82*	*0.96*
Northern Waterthrush	0.00	0.02	0.01
Louisiana Waterthrush	0.00	0.06	0.03
Common Yellowthroat	*0.80*	*0.94*	*0.87*
Scarlet Tanager	0.20	0.29	0.25
Eastern Towhee	**0.30**	**0.27**	**0.29**
Chipping Sparrow	0.45	0.27	0.36
Field Sparrow	***0.55***	***0.67***	***0.61***
Vesper Sparrow	0.00	0.06	0.03
Savannah Sparrow	0.00	0.04	0.02
Song Sparrow	*1.20*	*0.65*	*0.92*
Northern Cardinal	0.15	0.24	0.19
Rose-breasted Grosbeak	0.05	0.12	0.08
Indigo Bunting	0.00	0.06	0.03
Bobolink	*0.60*	*0.65*	*0.62*
Red-winged Blackbird	*0.70*	*1.82*	*1.26*
Eastern Meadowlark	0.15	0.43	0.29
Brown-headed Cowbird	0.05	0.06	0.05
Baltimore Oriole	**0.25**	**0.16**	**0.20**
American Goldfinch	*1.10*	*0.94*	*1.02*
Points Surveyed:	20	51	
Birds per Point:	15.90	16.27	16.09
Species Richness:	48	64	68
Shannon Diversity:	3.444	3.606	

Vanderbilt Mansion National Historic Site

Common Name	2007	2008	Mean
Canada Goose	*0.29*	*0.29*	*0.29*
Mourning Dove	0.00	0.14	0.07
Red-bellied Woodpecker	*1.00*	*0.14*	*0.57*
Downy Woodpecker	0.14	0.14	0.14
Hairy Woodpecker	0.29	0.00	0.14
Northern Flicker (Yellow-shafted Flicker)	0.14	0.00	0.07
Pileated Woodpecker	0.00	0.14	0.07
Eastern Phoebe	0.00	0.29	0.14
Great Crested Flycatcher	*0.71*	*0.57*	*0.64*
Red-eyed Vireo	*1.29*	*0.57*	*0.93*
Blue Jay	0.43	0.00	0.21
American Crow	*0.43*	*0.29*	*0.36*
Tufted Titmouse	*0.57*	*0.29*	*0.43*
White-breasted Nuthatch	*0.71*	*0.00*	*0.36*
Carolina Wren	*0.00*	*0.57*	*0.29*
House Wren	0.14	0.14	0.14
Wood Thrush	***1.14***	***0.57***	***0.86***
American Robin	0.00	0.29	0.14
American Redstart	0.29	0.00	0.14

Appendix A. Summary of species detected during monitoring activities in Northeast Temperate Network parks (continued).

Common Name	2007	2008	Mean
Worm-eating Warbler	**0.29**	**0.14**	**0.21**
Ovenbird	0.14	0.29	0.21
Scarlet Tanager	0.00	0.14	0.07
Chipping Sparrow	0.14	0.14	0.14
Northern Cardinal	*0.86*	*0.86*	*0.86*
Indigo Bunting	0.00	0.14	0.07
Points Surveyed:	7	7	
Birds per Point:	9.00	6.14	7.57
Species Richness:	18	20	25
Shannon Diversity:	2.642	2.802	

Appendix B. Summary results of breeding landbird monitoring for each Northeast Temperate Network Park (when more than one site was surveyed for a park).

This appendix contains the species list for each site (when more than one site was surveyed for a park), and the relative abundance (birds per point) of each species for each year. It only includes data for the first survey of each point in a given year, in order to promote more consistent comparisons between years and to avoid artificially inflating abundances due to counting the same individuals in repeat visits. Species in boldface are species of regional or continental concern, and species in italics are the 10 most common species for each park. There will occasionally be more than 10 italicized species, if multiple species have the same abundance.

This appendix also lists the number of points surveyed per site each year, the number of birds detected per point count, the species richness, and the Shannon diversity index for each site for each year.

Acadia National Park
Schoodic Peninsula

Common Name	*2007*	*2008*	*Mean*
Hairy Woodpecker	*0.67*		*0.67*
Least Flycatcher	*0.17*		*0.17*
Great Crested Flycatcher	*0.17*		*0.17*
American Crow	*0.17*		*0.17*
Boreal Chickadee	**1.00**		**1.00**
Red-breasted Nuthatch	*0.17*		*0.17*
Ruby-crowned Kinglet	*0.33*		*0.33*
Hermit Thrush	*0.67*		*0.67*
Wood Thrush	**0.17**		**0.17**
American Robin	*0.33*		*0.33*
Chestnut-sided Warbler	*0.33*		*0.33*
Black-throated Blue Warbler	*0.33*		*0.33*
Yellow-rumped Warbler (Myrtle Warbler)	*0.17*		*0.17*
Black-throated Green Warbler	*1.00*		*1.00*
Black-and-white Warbler	*0.17*		*0.17*
Eastern Towhee	**0.17**		**0.17**
Dark-eyed Junco (Slate-colored Junco)	*0.33*		*0.33*

Points Surveyed:	6	
Birds per Point:	6.33	6.33
Species Richness:	17	17
Shannon Diversity:	2.598	

Appendix B. Summary results of breeding landbird monitoring for each Northeast Temperate Network Park (when more than one site was surveyed for a park) (continued).

Acadia National Park
Giant Slide Trail

Common Name	2007	2008	Mean
Common Loon	0.00	0.10	0.05
Mourning Dove	*0.44*	*0.30*	*0.37*
Hairy Woodpecker	0.11	0.00	0.06
Pileated Woodpecker	0.11	0.10	0.11
Alder Flycatcher	0.11	0.00	0.06
Blue-headed Vireo	*0.78*	*0.50*	*0.64*
Blue Jay	0.44	0.10	0.27
American Crow	*0.33*	*0.50*	*0.42*
Common Raven	0.22	0.00	0.11
Black-capped Chickadee	0.11	0.60	0.36
Red-breasted Nuthatch	*0.67*	*0.40*	*0.53*
Brown Creeper	0.11	0.40	0.26
Winter Wren	0.22	0.10	0.16
Golden-crowned Kinglet	*0.67*	*1.40*	*1.03*
Hermit Thrush	0.22	0.10	0.16
American Robin	*0.89*	*0.70*	*0.79*
Brown Thrasher	0.11	0.00	0.06
Cedar Waxwing	0.33	0.10	0.22
Black-throated Blue Warbler	0.00	0.70	0.35
Yellow-rumped Warbler (Myrtle Warbler)	0.11	0.30	0.21
Black-throated Green Warbler	*2.78*	*2.90*	*2.84*
Blackburnian Warbler	*0.33*	*0.50*	*0.42*
Black-and-white Warbler	0.33	0.10	0.22
Ovenbird	*1.11*	*2.30*	*1.71*
Dark-eyed Junco (Slate-colored Junco)	0.11	0.10	0.11
Purple Finch	0.11	0.10	0.11
Pine Siskin	*0.56*	*1.00*	*0.78*
Points Surveyed:	9	10	
Birds per Point:	11.33	13.40	12.37
Species Richness:	25	23	27
Shannon Diversity:	2.745	2.588	

Appendix B. Summary results of breeding landbird monitoring for each Northeast Temperate Network Park (when more than one site was surveyed for a park) (continued).

Acadia National Park
Seal Cove Center

Common Name	2007	2008	Mean
Mourning Dove	1.00	1.33	1.17
Hairy Woodpecker	0.17	0.00	0.08
Pileated Woodpecker	0.50	0.00	0.25
Least Flycatcher	0.50	0.33	0.42
Blue-headed Vireo	0.33	1.00	0.67
Blue Jay	0.00	0.17	0.08
American Crow	0.17	0.00	0.08
Common Raven	0.50	0.00	0.25
Black-capped Chickadee	0.33	0.17	0.25
Red-breasted Nuthatch	0.50	0.17	0.33
Brown Creeper	0.17	0.00	0.08
Winter Wren	0.33	0.17	0.25
Golden-crowned Kinglet	0.17	0.50	0.33
Swainson's Thrush	0.33	0.00	0.17
Hermit Thrush	0.50	0.00	0.25
Magnolia Warbler	0.33	0.17	0.25
Black-throated Green Warbler	1.33	1.00	1.17
Blackburnian Warbler	0.17	0.33	0.25
Ovenbird	0.33	0.50	0.42
Dark-eyed Junco (Slate-colored Junco)	0.17	0.17	0.17
Purple Finch	0.50	0.17	0.33
Pine Siskin	0.00	0.33	0.17
Points Surveyed:	6	6	
Birds per Point:	8.33	6.50	7.42
Species Richness:	20	15	22
Shannon Diversity:	2.802	2.410	

Appendix B. Summary results of breeding landbird monitoring for each Northeast Temperate Network Park (when more than one site was surveyed for a park) (continued).

Acadia National Park
Seal Cove East

Common Name	2007	2008	Mean
Herring Gull	0.14	0.00	0.07
Mourning Dove	*1.14*	*0.43*	*0.79*
Pileated Woodpecker	0.14	0.14	0.14
Blue-headed Vireo	0.14	0.43	0.29
Red-eyed Vireo	0.00	0.14	0.07
Blue Jay	0.14	0.29	0.21
American Crow	*0.86*	*0.86*	*0.86*
Common Raven	*0.57*	*0.29*	*0.43*
Black-capped Chickadee	0.14	0.14	0.14
Red-breasted Nuthatch	*0.57*	*0.14*	*0.36*
Brown Creeper	0.00	0.57	0.29
Winter Wren	*0.43*	*0.43*	*0.43*
Golden-crowned Kinglet	*0.43*	*0.29*	*0.36*
Swainson's Thrush	0.29	0.14	0.21
Hermit Thrush	0.14	0.00	0.07
American Robin	0.43	0.00	0.21
Northern Parula	0.14	0.00	0.07
Magnolia Warbler	*0.29*	*0.43*	*0.36*
Yellow-rumped Warbler (Myrtle Warbler)	*0.14*	*0.57*	*0.36*
Black-throated Green Warbler	*1.43*	*1.14*	*1.29*
Blackburnian Warbler	*0.57*	*0.29*	*0.43*
Blackpoll Warbler	**0.00**	**0.14**	**0.07**
Ovenbird	*1.00*	*1.00*	*1.00*
Common Yellowthroat	0.00	0.14	0.07
Dark-eyed Junco (Slate-colored Junco)	0.29	0.29	0.29
Red-winged Blackbird	0.14	0.29	0.21
Common Grackle	0.14	0.00	0.07
Purple Finch	0.14	0.14	0.14
Pine Siskin	*0.43*	*0.43*	*0.43*

	2007	2008	Mean
Points Surveyed:	7	7	
Birds per Point:	10.29	9.14	9.71
Species Richness:	25	24	29
Shannon Diversity:	2.915	2.957	

Appendix B. Summary results of breeding landbird monitoring for each Northeast Temperate Network Park (when more than one site was surveyed for a park) (continued).

Marsh-Billings-Rockefeller National Historical Park
East

Common Name	2007	2008	Mean
Mourning Dove	0.00	0.10	0.05
Barred Owl	0.10	0.00	0.05
Yellow-bellied Sapsucker	0.30	0.30	0.30
Downy Woodpecker	0.10	0.00	0.05
Hairy Woodpecker	0.20	0.30	0.25
Pileated Woodpecker	0.10	0.00	0.05
Eastern Wood-Pewee	0.30	0.20	0.25
Great Crested Flycatcher	0.10	0.10	0.10
Blue-headed Vireo	0.10	0.30	0.20
Red-eyed Vireo	*1.80*	*1.70*	*1.75*
Blue Jay	*0.80*	*0.40*	*0.60*
American Crow	*0.40*	*0.20*	*0.30*
Black-capped Chickadee	*1.10*	*0.40*	*0.75*
Tufted Titmouse	0.00	0.10	0.05
White-breasted Nuthatch	0.20	0.10	0.15
Brown Creeper	*0.50*	*0.40*	*0.45*
Winter Wren	0.00	0.40	0.20
Veery	0.10	0.00	0.05
Hermit Thrush	*0.70*	*1.00*	*0.85*
Wood Thrush	**0.00**	**0.30**	**0.15**
American Robin	*0.40*	*0.20*	*0.30*
Black-throated Blue Warbler	0.10	0.00	0.05
Black-throated Green Warbler	*0.70*	*0.50*	*0.60*
Blackburnian Warbler	*0.70*	*0.70*	*0.70*
Pine Warbler	0.10	0.20	0.15
Black-and-white Warbler	0.10	0.00	0.05
Ovenbird	*3.60*	*3.20*	*3.40*
Louisiana Waterthrush	0.20	0.00	0.10
Common Yellowthroat	0.10	0.10	0.10
Scarlet Tanager	*0.20*	*0.40*	*0.30*
Dark-eyed Junco (Slate-colored Junco)	0.30	0.00	0.15
Indigo Bunting	0.20	0.00	0.10
Brown-headed Cowbird	0.10	0.10	0.10
American Goldfinch	0.10	0.00	0.05
Points Surveyed:	10	10	
Birds per Point:	13.80	11.70	12.75
Species Richness:	30	24	34
Shannon Diversity:	2.747	2.624	

Appendix B. Summary results of breeding landbird monitoring for each Northeast Temperate Network Park (when more than one site was surveyed for a park) (continued).

Marsh-Billings-Rockefeller National Historical Park
Northwest

Common Name	2007	2008	Mean
Mourning Dove	0.20	0.20	0.20
Yellow-bellied Sapsucker	0.30	0.00	0.15
Downy Woodpecker	0.10	0.00	0.05
Hairy Woodpecker	0.30	0.20	0.25
Northern Flicker (Yellow-shafted Flicker)	0.10	0.00	0.05
Eastern Wood-Pewee	*0.80*	*1.40*	*1.10*
Great Crested Flycatcher	*0.00*	*0.80*	*0.40*
Blue-headed Vireo	0.30	0.00	0.15
Red-eyed Vireo	*1.70*	*3.80*	*2.75*
Blue Jay	*0.60*	*0.60*	*0.60*
American Crow	0.30	0.20	0.25
Common Raven	0.00	0.20	0.10
Black-capped Chickadee	*0.40*	*0.60*	*0.50*
Red-breasted Nuthatch	0.20	0.00	0.10
White-breasted Nuthatch	0.20	0.00	0.10
Brown Creeper	0.50	0.20	0.35
Winter Wren	0.10	0.00	0.05
Golden-crowned Kinglet	0.10	0.00	0.05
Veery	0.10	0.40	0.25
Hermit Thrush	*0.40*	*0.80*	*0.60*
Wood Thrush	***0.60***	***0.60***	***0.60***
American Robin	0.40	0.20	0.30
Cedar Waxwing	0.00	0.20	0.10
Black-throated Blue Warbler	*0.50*	*0.60*	*0.55*
Black-throated Green Warbler	*0.60*	*1.20*	*0.90*
Blackburnian Warbler	0.70	0.00	0.35
American Redstart	0.10	0.00	0.05
Ovenbird	*2.60*	*4.80*	*3.70*
Scarlet Tanager	*0.80*	*0.00*	*0.40*
Dark-eyed Junco (Slate-colored Junco)	0.20	0.00	0.10
Rose-breasted Grosbeak	0.10	0.00	0.05
Common Grackle	0.10	0.00	0.05
Brown-headed Cowbird	0.10	0.00	0.05
Purple Finch	0.10	0.00	0.05
Points Surveyed:	10	5	
Birds per Point:	13.60	17.00	15.30
Species Richness:	31	18	34
Shannon Diversity:	2.975	2.299	

Appendix B. Summary results of breeding landbird monitoring for each Northeast Temperate Network Park (when more than one site was surveyed for a park) (continued).

Marsh-Billings-Rockefeller National Historical Park
South

Common Name	2007	2008	Mean
Wild Turkey	0.00	0.20	0.10
Mourning Dove	0.40	0.20	0.30
Barred Owl	1.20	0.00	0.60
Yellow-bellied Sapsucker	0.40	0.20	0.30
Downy Woodpecker	0.20	0.00	0.10
Eastern Wood-Pewee	*1.40*	*0.40*	*0.90*
Least Flycatcher	0.60	0.20	0.40
Eastern Kingbird	0.20	0.00	0.10
Blue-headed Vireo	0.20	0.20	0.20
Red-eyed Vireo	*2.00*	*0.20*	*1.10*
Blue Jay	*1.40*	*0.20*	*0.80*
American Crow	0.40	0.00	0.20
Black-capped Chickadee	*1.20*	*0.60*	*0.90*
Tufted Titmouse	0.20	0.00	0.10
White-breasted Nuthatch	0.80	0.20	0.50
Brown Creeper	*0.80*	*0.60*	*0.70*
Golden-crowned Kinglet	0.00	0.20	0.10
Veery	0.20	0.00	0.10
Hermit Thrush	*1.40*	*1.40*	*1.40*
Wood Thrush	**0.00**	**0.20**	**0.10**
American Robin	*1.60*	*0.80*	*1.20*
Cedar Waxwing	0.20	0.00	0.10
Chestnut-sided Warbler	0.00	0.20	0.10
Yellow-rumped Warbler (Myrtle Warbler)	0.40	0.20	0.30
Black-throated Green Warbler	1.00	0.20	0.60
Blackburnian Warbler	0.60	0.60	0.60
Black-and-white Warbler	0.20	0.00	0.10
Ovenbird	*4.40*	*2.60*	*3.50*
Common Yellowthroat	0.40	0.60	0.50
Scarlet Tanager	0.80	0.20	0.50
Chipping Sparrow	0.20	0.00	0.10
Dark-eyed Junco (Slate-colored Junco)	*1.20*	*0.20*	*0.70*
Rose-breasted Grosbeak	0.40	0.20	0.30
Indigo Bunting	0.60	0.40	0.50
Bobolink	**0.20**	**0.00**	**0.10**
Red-winged Blackbird	*1.40*	*0.60*	*1.00*
American Goldfinch	0.00	0.20	0.10

	2007	2008	Mean
Points Surveyed:	5	5	
Birds per Point:	26.60	12.00	19.30
Species Richness:	32	27	37
Shannon Diversity:	3.106	2.898	

Appendix B. Summary results of breeding landbird monitoring for each Northeast Temperate Network Park (when more than one site was surveyed for a park) (continued).

Minute Man National Historical Park
Hartwell Tavern

Common Name	2007	2008	Mean
Black-billed Cuckoo	**0.00**	**0.14**	**0.07**
Red-bellied Woodpecker	0.29	0.29	0.29
Downy Woodpecker	*0.71*	*0.57*	*0.64*
Hairy Woodpecker	0.29	0.00	0.14
Northern Flicker (Yellow-shafted Flicker)	0.00	0.14	0.07
Eastern Wood-Pewee	***0.86***	***0.43***	***0.64***
Eastern Phoebe	0.00	0.14	0.07
Great Crested Flycatcher	0.00	0.43	0.21
Red-eyed Vireo	*0.29*	*0.71*	*0.50*
Blue Jay	*0.86*	*1.43*	*1.14*
American Crow	*1.00*	*1.29*	*1.14*
Black-capped Chickadee	*0.71*	*0.86*	*0.79*
Tufted Titmouse	*1.86*	*2.57*	*2.21*
White-breasted Nuthatch	*0.57*	*0.43*	*0.50*
Carolina Wren	0.14	0.00	0.07
Wood Thrush	**0.14**	**0.57**	**0.36**
American Robin	*1.00*	*2.14*	*1.57*
Gray Catbird	0.14	0.57	0.36
Cedar Waxwing	0.14	0.00	0.07
Yellow Warbler	0.00	0.14	0.07
Pine Warbler	0.14	0.00	0.07
Ovenbird	*0.86*	*0.43*	*0.64*
Common Yellowthroat	0.29	0.57	0.43
Scarlet Tanager	**0.29**	**0.57**	**0.43**
Chipping Sparrow	0.00	0.43	0.21
Song Sparrow	0.14	0.14	0.14
Northern Cardinal	*0.57*	*1.00*	*0.79*
Rose-breasted Grosbeak	**0.14**	**0.00**	**0.07**
Indigo Bunting	0.00	0.29	0.14
Red-winged Blackbird	0.00	0.14	0.07
Common Grackle	0.14	0.14	0.14
Brown-headed Cowbird	0.43	0.29	0.36
Baltimore Oriole	**0.14**	**0.00**	**0.07**
American Goldfinch	0.29	0.29	0.29

	2007	2008	Mean
Points Surveyed:	7	7	
Birds per Point:	12.43	17.14	14.79
Species Richness:	26	28	34
Shannon Diversity:	2.953	2.974	

Minute Man National Historical Park
Miriam's Corner

Common Name	2007	2008	Mean
Canada Goose	0.13	0.00	0.06
Mourning Dove	0.00	0.25	0.13
Chimney Swift	**0.25**	**0.00**	**0.13**
Downy Woodpecker	*0.88*	*0.38*	*0.63*
Hairy Woodpecker	0.25	0.00	0.13
Northern Flicker (Yellow-shafted Flicker)	0.00	0.25	0.13
Great Crested Flycatcher	0.00	0.25	0.13
Warbling Vireo	0.00	0.13	0.06
Red-eyed Vireo	0.00	0.13	0.06
Blue Jay	*0.75*	*0.50*	*0.63*
American Crow	0.63	0.38	0.50
Black-capped Chickadee	*1.00*	*0.25*	*0.63*
Tufted Titmouse	*0.88*	*0.50*	*0.69*
White-breasted Nuthatch	0.13	0.00	0.06
Carolina Wren	0.13	0.00	0.06
Veery	**0.38**	**0.00**	**0.19**
Wood Thrush	***0.75***	***0.50***	***0.63***
American Robin	1.00	0.00	0.50
Gray Catbird	*0.88*	*0.25*	*0.56*
Northern Mockingbird	0.25	0.00	0.13
Yellow Warbler	0.00	0.25	0.13
Pine Warbler	0.50	0.25	0.38
American Redstart	0.13	0.00	0.06
Ovenbird	*0.75*	*0.50*	*0.63*
Common Yellowthroat	*1.00*	*0.25*	*0.63*
Scarlet Tanager	**0.00**	**0.13**	**0.06**
Song Sparrow	*0.88*	*0.63*	*0.75*
Swamp Sparrow	0.00	0.13	0.06
Northern Cardinal	*0.63*	*0.50*	*0.56*
Rose-breasted Grosbeak	**0.38**	**0.38**	**0.38**
Indigo Bunting	0.38	0.13	0.25
Red-winged Blackbird	0.13	0.50	0.31
Brown-headed Cowbird	0.50	0.13	0.31
Baltimore Oriole	**0.25**	**0.00**	**0.13**
House Finch	0.00	0.13	0.06
American Goldfinch	0.63	0.25	0.44
House Sparrow	0.25	0.00	0.13
Points Surveyed:	8	8	
Birds per Point:	14.63	7.88	11.25
Species Richness:	28	26	37
Shannon Diversity:	3.149	3.132	

Appendix B. Summary results of breeding landbird monitoring for each Northeast Temperate Network Park (when more than one site was surveyed for a park) (continued).

Minute Man NHP
The Bluff

Common Name	2007	2008	Mean
Red-bellied Woodpecker	0.00	0.13	0.06
Red-eyed Vireo	0.00	0.25	0.13
Blue Jay	*1.75*	*1.75*	*1.75*
American Crow	*0.63*	*0.88*	*0.75*
Black-capped Chickadee	*0.25*	*0.38*	*0.31*
Tufted Titmouse	*1.75*	*1.38*	*1.56*
White-breasted Nuthatch	0.50	0.00	0.25
Carolina Wren	0.25	0.00	0.13
House Wren	0.13	0.00	0.06
American Robin	*0.75*	*1.38*	*1.06*
Gray Catbird	*0.38*	*0.63*	*0.50*
Pine Warbler	*0.25*	*0.88*	*0.56*
Common Yellowthroat	0.00	0.25	0.13
Chipping Sparrow	0.00	0.13	0.06
Song Sparrow	*0.75*	*0.63*	*0.69*
Northern Cardinal	*1.00*	*0.63*	*0.81*
Red-winged Blackbird	*1.13*	*0.75*	*0.94*
Common Grackle	0.25	0.13	0.19
Brown-headed Cowbird	0.50	0.00	0.25
House Finch	0.25	0.00	0.13
American Goldfinch	*0.50*	*0.13*	*0.31*
House Sparrow	0.13	0.13	0.13
Points Surveyed:	8	8	
Birds per Point:	11.13	10.38	10.75
Species Richness:	18	17	22
Shannon Diversity:	2.615	2.516	

Appendix B. Summary results of breeding landbird monitoring for each Northeast Temperate Network Park (when more than one site was surveyed for a park) (continued).

Morristown NHP
Mt. Kemble

Common Name	2007	2008	Mean
Red-tailed Hawk		0.20	0.20
Mourning Dove		0.30	0.30
Yellow-billed Cuckoo		0.10	0.10
Great Horned Owl		0.20	0.20
Red-bellied Woodpecker		*0.60*	*0.60*
Downy Woodpecker		*0.60*	*0.60*
Hairy Woodpecker		0.50	0.50
Northern Flicker (Yellow-shafted Flicker)		0.40	0.40
Pileated Woodpecker		0.20	0.20
Eastern Wood-Pewee		***1.10***	***1.10***
Eastern Phoebe		0.10	0.10
Great Crested Flycatcher		0.20	0.20
Red-eyed Vireo		0.20	0.20
Blue Jay		*1.30*	*1.30*
American Crow		*0.70*	*0.70*
Black-capped Chickadee		0.10	0.10
Tufted Titmouse		*1.00*	*1.00*
White-breasted Nuthatch		*0.80*	*0.80*
House Wren		0.10	0.10
Eastern Bluebird		0.20	0.20
Veery		0.40	0.40
Wood Thrush		***1.50***	***1.50***
American Robin		*0.90*	*0.90*
Gray Catbird		0.10	0.10
Worm-eating Warbler		**0.40**	**0.40**
Ovenbird		*0.60*	*0.60*
Scarlet Tanager		0.50	0.50
Northern Cardinal		0.10	0.10
Rose-breasted Grosbeak		0.10	0.10
Indigo Bunting		0.20	0.20
Points Surveyed:	10		
Birds per Point:	13.70	13.70	
Species Richness:	30	30	
Shannon Diversity:	3.085		

Morristown NHP
Primrose Brook

Common Name	2007	2008	Mean
Wild Turkey	0.20	0.00	0.10
Red-tailed Hawk	0.10	0.00	0.05
Mourning Dove	0.10	0.00	0.05
Yellow-billed Cuckoo	0.40	0.00	0.20
Red-bellied Woodpecker	*0.40*	*1.20*	*0.80*
Downy Woodpecker	0.10	0.00	0.05
Northern Flicker (Yellow-shafted Flicker)	0.70	0.10	0.40
Pileated Woodpecker	0.10	0.00	0.05
Eastern Wood-Pewee	**0.80**	**0.20**	**0.50**
Eastern Phoebe	0.10	0.00	0.05
Great Crested Flycatcher	0.00	0.20	0.10
Yellow-throated Vireo	**0.00**	**0.10**	**0.05**
Red-eyed Vireo	*1.10*	*0.50*	*0.80*
Blue Jay	*1.70*	*0.90*	*1.30*
American Crow	0.80	0.10	0.45
Black-capped Chickadee	0.10	0.00	0.05
Tufted Titmouse	*0.50*	*0.80*	*0.65*
White-breasted Nuthatch	0.50	0.40	0.45
Carolina Wren	0.20	0.00	0.10
Eastern Bluebird	0.00	0.10	0.05
Veery	*0.70*	*0.60*	*0.65*
Wood Thrush	**1.90**	**0.90**	**1.40**
American Robin	*1.30*	*1.00*	*1.15*
Gray Catbird	0.00	0.10	0.05
Worm-eating Warbler	**0.40**	**0.00**	**0.20**
Ovenbird	*1.10*	*0.40*	*0.75*
Louisiana Waterthrush	**0.10**	**0.00**	**0.05**
Hooded Warbler	0.20	0.00	0.10
Scarlet Tanager	*1.20*	*0.50*	*0.85*
Eastern Towhee	**0.40**	**0.10**	**0.25**
Northern Cardinal	*0.90*	*0.10*	*0.50*
Rose-breasted Grosbeak	0.10	0.10	0.10
Brown-headed Cowbird	0.10	0.00	0.05
Baltimore Oriole	0.10	0.60	0.35
Points Surveyed:	10	10	
Birds per Point:	16.40	9.00	12.70
Species Richness:	30	21	34
Shannon Diversity:	3.010	2.717	

Appendix B. Summary results of breeding landbird monitoring for each Northeast Temperate Network Park (when more than one site was surveyed for a park) (continued).

Morristown NHP
Soldier's Huts

Common Name	2007	2008	Mean
Red-bellied Woodpecker	0.11		0.11
Downy Woodpecker	0.11		0.11
Northern Flicker (Yellow-shafted Flicker)	*0.33*		*0.33*
Pileated Woodpecker	0.11		0.11
Eastern Wood-Pewee	**1.00**		**1.00**
Great Crested Flycatcher	0.11		0.11
Yellow-throated Vireo	**0.22**		**0.22**
Red-eyed Vireo	*0.89*		*0.89*
Blue Jay	*0.33*		*0.33*
American Crow	0.11		0.11
Tufted Titmouse	*0.44*		*0.44*
Veery	*0.78*		*0.78*
Wood Thrush	**1.22**		**1.22**
American Robin	*0.78*		*0.78*
Gray Catbird	0.22		0.22
American Redstart	*0.67*		*0.67*
Ovenbird	*1.11*		*1.11*
Louisiana Waterthrush	**0.11**		**0.11**
Kentucky Warbler	**0.11**		**0.11**
Hooded Warbler	0.22		0.22
Scarlet Tanager	*0.33*		*0.33*
Eastern Towhee	**0.67**		**0.67**
Chipping Sparrow	0.11		0.11
Rose-breasted Grosbeak	*0.33*		*0.33*
Brown-headed Cowbird	0.22		0.22
Baltimore Oriole	0.11		0.11
Points Surveyed:	9		
Birds per Point:	10.78		10.78
Species Richness:	26		26
Shannon Diversity:	2.937		

Appendix B. Summary results of breeding landbird monitoring for each Northeast Temperate Network Park (when more than one site was surveyed for a park) (continued).

Saratoga National Historical Park
Middle Ravine

Common Name	2007	2008	Mean
Canada Goose	0.00	0.10	0.05
Mourning Dove	*0.70*	*0.60*	*0.65*
Yellow-bellied Sapsucker	0.10	0.30	0.20
Downy Woodpecker	0.20	0.50	0.35
Northern Flicker (Yellow-shafted Flicker)	0.20	0.00	0.10
Eastern Wood-Pewee	***0.40***	***0.80***	***0.60***
Eastern Phoebe	0.10	0.00	0.05
Great Crested Flycatcher	0.50	0.50	0.50
Red-eyed Vireo	*0.60*	*0.70*	*0.65*
Blue Jay	*0.50*	*0.60*	*0.55*
American Crow	0.60	0.40	0.50
Black-capped Chickadee	*1.00*	*0.70*	*0.85*
Tufted Titmouse	0.30	0.40	0.35
Red-breasted Nuthatch	0.00	0.10	0.05
White-breasted Nuthatch	0.20	0.10	0.15
Brown Creeper	0.10	0.30	0.20
Winter Wren	0.10	0.00	0.05
Veery	0.20	0.30	0.25
Hermit Thrush	0.10	0.40	0.25
Wood Thrush	***0.80***	***0.30***	***0.55***
American Robin	*1.40*	*0.50*	*0.95*
Cedar Waxwing	0.40	0.00	0.20
Blue-winged Warbler	**0.00**	**0.10**	**0.05**
Golden-winged Warbler	**0.10**	**0.00**	**0.05**
Chestnut-sided Warbler	0.10	0.00	0.05
Yellow-rumped Warbler (Myrtle Warbler)	0.00	0.20	0.10
American Redstart	0.10	0.00	0.05
Ovenbird	*1.80*	*1.30*	*1.55*
Common Yellowthroat	*0.80*	*0.80*	*0.80*
Scarlet Tanager	0.40	0.40	0.40
Eastern Towhee	***0.60***	***0.50***	***0.55***
Chipping Sparrow	0.20	0.00	0.10
Field Sparrow	**0.20**	**0.20**	**0.20**
Song Sparrow	0.40	0.30	0.35
Northern Cardinal	0.10	0.40	0.25
Rose-breasted Grosbeak	0.10	0.20	0.15
Red-winged Blackbird	0.20	0.40	0.30
Brown-headed Cowbird	0.10	0.20	0.15
Baltimore Oriole	**0.10**	**0.00**	**0.05**
American Goldfinch	*1.10*	*1.20*	*1.15*
Points Surveyed:	10	10	
Birds per Point:	14.90	13.80	14.35
Species Richness:	36	31	40
Shannon Diversity:	3.200	3.241	

Appendix B. Summary results of breeding landbird monitoring for each Northeast Temperate Network Park (when more than one site was surveyed for a park) (continued).

Saratoga National Historical Park
Wilkinson Trail

Common Name	2007	2008	Mean
Canada Goose		0.10	0.10
Mourning Dove		0.10	0.10
Black-billed Cuckoo		**0.10**	**0.10**
Yellow-billed Cuckoo		0.10	0.10
Yellow-bellied Sapsucker		0.20	0.20
Downy Woodpecker		0.30	0.30
Pileated Woodpecker		0.10	0.10
Eastern Wood-Pewee		*1.20*	*1.20*
Acadian Flycatcher		0.10	0.10
Least Flycatcher		0.20	0.20
Eastern Phoebe		0.30	0.30
Great Crested Flycatcher		*0.90*	*0.90*
Red-eyed Vireo		*1.20*	*1.20*
Blue Jay		0.30	0.30
American Crow		0.50	0.50
Black-capped Chickadee		*1.20*	*1.20*
Tufted Titmouse		0.40	0.40
Red-breasted Nuthatch		0.10	0.10
White-breasted Nuthatch		0.10	0.10
Brown Creeper		0.40	0.40
Blue-gray Gnatcatcher		0.10	0.10
Veery		0.20	0.20
Wood Thrush		***0.60***	***0.60***
American Robin		*0.60*	*0.60*
Gray Catbird		0.40	0.40
Chestnut-sided Warbler		0.40	0.40
Ovenbird		*1.70*	*1.70*
Northern Waterthrush		0.10	0.10
Louisiana Waterthrush		0.20	0.20
Common Yellowthroat		*0.90*	*0.90*
Scarlet Tanager		*0.60*	*0.60*
Eastern Towhee		**0.10**	**0.10**
Chipping Sparrow		0.20	0.20
Song Sparrow		0.10	0.10
Northern Cardinal		0.10	0.10
Rose-breasted Grosbeak		0.20	0.20
Indigo Bunting		0.20	0.20
American Goldfinch		*0.60*	*0.60*
Points Surveyed:		10	
Birds per Point:		15.20	15.20
Species Richness:		38	38
Shannon Diversity:		3.248	

Appendix B. Summary results of breeding landbird monitoring for each Northeast Temperate Network Park (when more than one site was surveyed for a park) (continued).

Saratoga National Historical Park
Bemis Heights

Common Name	2007	2008	Mean
Mourning Dove		0.33	0.33
Yellow-bellied Sapsucker		0.17	0.17
Pileated Woodpecker		0.17	0.17
Eastern Wood-Pewee		**0.50**	**0.50**
Alder Flycatcher		0.17	0.17
Eastern Phoebe		0.17	0.17
Red-eyed Vireo		0.83	0.83
Blue Jay		0.83	0.83
American Crow		0.17	0.17
Black-capped Chickadee		0.83	0.83
Tufted Titmouse		1.17	1.17
White-breasted Nuthatch		0.17	0.17
Blue-gray Gnatcatcher		0.33	0.33
Veery		0.67	0.67
Wood Thrush		**1.83**	**1.83**
American Robin		0.67	0.67
Cedar Waxwing		0.33	0.33
Blue-winged Warbler		**0.17**	**0.17**
Chestnut-sided Warbler		0.17	0.17
Black-and-white Warbler		0.33	0.33
Ovenbird		1.33	1.33
Louisiana Waterthrush		0.17	0.17
Common Yellowthroat		1.33	1.33
Scarlet Tanager		0.83	0.83
Eastern Towhee		**0.33**	**0.33**
Chipping Sparrow		0.17	0.17
Brown-headed Cowbird		0.17	0.17
American Goldfinch		0.67	0.67

	2007	2008
Points Surveyed:	6	
Birds per Point:	15.00	15.00
Species Richness:	28	28
Shannon Diversity:	3.030	

Appendix B. Summary results of breeding landbird monitoring for each Northeast Temperate Network Park (when more than one site was surveyed for a park) (continued).

Saratoga National Historical Park
Burgoyne's Headquarters

Common Name	2007	2008	Mean
Canada Goose		0.20	0.20
Mourning Dove		*0.60*	*0.60*
Black-billed Cuckoo		0.20	0.20
Red-bellied Woodpecker		0.20	0.20
Yellow-bellied Sapsucker		0.20	0.20
Downy Woodpecker		0.20	0.20
Eastern Wood-Pewee		0.40	0.40
Alder Flycatcher		0.20	0.20
Least Flycatcher		0.40	0.40
Eastern Kingbird		*0.60*	*0.60*
Warbling Vireo		0.20	0.20
Blue Jay		0.20	0.20
American Crow		0.20	0.20
Tree Swallow		*1.00*	*1.00*
American Robin		*0.80*	*0.80*
Gray Catbird		0.20	0.20
Cedar Waxwing		*0.60*	*0.60*
Blue-winged Warbler		*0.60*	*0.60*
Yellow Warbler		0.20	0.20
Common Yellowthroat		*1.00*	*1.00*
Chipping Sparrow		*0.80*	*0.80*
Field Sparrow		*2.00*	*2.00*
Vesper Sparrow		0.40	0.40
Savannah Sparrow		0.40	0.40
Song Sparrow		*1.00*	*1.00*
Rose-breasted Grosbeak		0.20	0.20
Indigo Bunting		0.20	0.20
Red-winged Blackbird		*2.40*	*2.40*
Eastern Meadowlark		0.40	0.40
Baltimore Oriole		0.40	0.40
American Goldfinch		*1.80*	*1.80*
Points Surveyed:		5	
Birds per Point:		18.20	18.20
Species Richness:		31	31
Shannon Diversity:		3.089	

Appendix B. Summary results of breeding landbird monitoring for each Northeast Temperate Network Park (when more than one site was surveyed for a park) (continued).

Saratoga National Historical Park
Freeman Farm

Common Name	2007	2008	Mean
Canada Goose	0.10	0.10	0.10
Great Blue Heron	0.10	0.00	0.05
Mourning Dove	0.40	0.50	0.45
Red-bellied Woodpecker	0.00	0.10	0.05
Downy Woodpecker	0.00	0.10	0.05
Northern Flicker (Yellow-shafted Flicker)	0.10	0.20	0.15
Eastern Wood-Pewee	0.20	0.30	0.25
Alder Flycatcher	0.10	0.10	0.10
Willow Flycatcher	0.00	0.10	0.05
Great Crested Flycatcher	0.60	0.40	0.50
Eastern Kingbird	0.20	0.30	0.25
Yellow-throated Vireo	0.10	0.10	0.10
Red-eyed Vireo	0.40	0.10	0.25
Blue Jay	0.30	0.20	0.25
American Crow	*0.90*	*0.90*	*0.90*
Tree Swallow	*0.80*	*0.30*	*0.55*
Black-capped Chickadee	0.40	0.00	0.20
Tufted Titmouse	0.30	0.10	0.20
White-breasted Nuthatch	0.10	0.00	0.05
House Wren	0.00	0.10	0.05
Eastern Bluebird	0.00	0.10	0.05
Hermit Thrush	0.00	0.10	0.05
Wood Thrush	0.20	0.00	0.10
American Robin	*0.40*	*0.70*	*0.55*
Gray Catbird	0.10	0.20	0.15
Cedar Waxwing	0.80	0.00	0.40
Blue-winged Warbler	0.40	0.10	0.25
Golden-winged Warbler	0.10	0.00	0.05
Yellow Warbler	0.20	0.30	0.25
Chestnut-sided Warbler	0.10	0.50	0.30
Prairie Warbler	0.30	0.30	0.30
Ovenbird	0.40	0.40	0.40
Common Yellowthroat	*0.80*	*0.80*	*0.80*
Eastern Towhee	0.00	0.40	0.20
Chipping Sparrow	*0.70*	*0.60*	*0.65*
Field Sparrow	*0.90*	*1.60*	*1.25*
Vesper Sparrow	0.00	0.10	0.05
Song Sparrow	*2.00*	*1.10*	*1.55*
Northern Cardinal	0.20	0.30	0.25
Bobolink	*1.20*	*1.10*	*1.15*
R ed-winged Blackbird	*1.20*	*2.10*	*1.65*
Eastern Meadowlark	0.30	0.70	0.50
Baltimore Oriole	0.40	0.20	0.30
American Goldfinch	*1.10*	*0.90*	*1.00*
Points Surveyed:	10	10	

70

	2007	2008	Mean
Birds per Point:	16.90	16.60	16.75
Species Richness:	36	38	44
Shannon Diversity:	3.244	3.225	

Saratoga National Historical Park
Neilson Farm

Common Name	2007	2008	Mean
American Kestrel		0.20	0.20
Mourning Dove		0.50	0.50
Eastern Wood-Pewee		0.20	0.20
Alder Flycatcher		0.10	0.10
Willow Flycatcher		*0.70*	*0.70*
Eastern Kingbird		0.20	0.20
Blue Jay		0.20	0.20
American Crow		*0.90*	*0.90*
Tree Swallow		0.20	0.20
American Robin		*0.60*	*0.60*
Gray Catbird		0.10	0.10
Cedar Waxwing		*0.60*	*0.60*
Blue-winged Warbler		0.40	0.40
Yellow Warbler		0.40	0.40
Common Yellowthroat		*1.00*	*1.00*
Eastern Towhee		0.20	0.20
Chipping Sparrow		0.10	0.10
Field Sparrow		*0.60*	*0.60*
Song Sparrow		*1.30*	*1.30*
Northern Cardinal		0.40	0.40
Rose-breasted Grosbeak		0.10	0.10
Bobolink		*2.20*	*2.20*
Red-winged Blackbird		*5.60*	*5.60*
Eastern Meadowlark		*1.30*	*1.30*
Baltimore Oriole		0.40	0.40
American Goldfinch		*0.80*	*0.80*
Points Surveyed:		10	
Birds per Point:		19.30	19.30
Species Richness:		26	26
Shannon Diversity:		2.651	

Appendix C. Index of Biotic Integrity (IBI) for each site (if the park has multiple sites). Please refer to the Introduction for some important caveats pertaining to the IBI.

2007 Acadia National Park – Schoodic Peninsula

Integrity Element: *Compositional*

Response Guild	Percentage	Rating
Exotic	0%	Good
Nest Predator / Brood Parasite	6%	Good
Resident	24%	Good
Single Brooded	53%	Caution

Integrity Element: *Functional*

Response Guild	Percentage	Rating
Bark Prober	18%	Good
Ground Gleaner	6%	Caution
High Canopy Forager	6%	Sig Concern
Low Canopy Forager	29%	Good
Omnivore	29%	Good

Integrity Element: *Structural*

Response Guild	Percentage	Rating
Canopy Nester	29%	Caution
Forest-ground Nester	24%	Good
Interior Forest Obligate	41%	Good
Shrub Nester	24%	Caution

2007 Acadia National Park - Giant Slide Trail

Integrity Element: *Compositional*

Response Guild	Percentage	Rating
Exotic	0%	Good
Nest Predator / Brood Parasite	12%	Caution
Resident	48%	Sig Concern
Single Brooded	56%	Caution

Integrity Element: *Functional*

Response Guild	Percentage	Rating
Bark Prober	20%	Good
Ground Gleaner	12%	Good
High Canopy Forager	8%	Caution
Low Canopy Forager	16%	Caution
Omnivore	28%	Good

Integrity Element: *Structural*

Response Guild	Percentage	Rating
Canopy Nester	44%	Good
Forest-ground Nester	16%	Caution
Interior Forest Obligate	48%	Good
Shrub Nester	12%	Good

2008   Acadia National Park - Giant Slide Trail

Integrity Element: *Compositional*

Response Guild	Percentage	Rating
Exotic	0%	Good
Nest Predator / Brood Parasite	9%	Good
Resident	43%	Sig Concern
Single Brooded	57%	Caution

Integrity Element: *Functional*

Response Guild	Percentage	Rating
Bark Prober	17%	Good
Ground Gleaner	13%	Good
High Canopy Forager	9%	Caution
Low Canopy Forager	22%	Caution
Omnivore	22%	Good

Integrity Element: *Structural*

Response Guild	Percentage	Rating
Canopy Nester	43%	Good
Forest-ground Nester	17%	Caution
Interior Forest Obligate	52%	Good
Shrub Nester	9%	Good

2007   Acadia National Park - Seal Cove Center

Integrity Element: *Compositional*

Response Guild	Percentage	Rating
Exotic	0%	Good
Nest Predator / Brood Parasite	10%	Caution
Resident	45%	Sig Concern
Single Brooded	65%	Caution

Integrity Element: *Functional*

Response Guild	Percentage	Rating
Bark Prober	20%	Good
Ground Gleaner	15%	Good
High Canopy Forager	10%	Caution
Low Canopy Forager	20%	Caution
Omnivore	20%	Good

Integrity Element: *Structural*

Response Guild	Percentage	Rating
Canopy Nester	45%	Good
Forest-ground Nester	15%	Caution
Interior Forest Obligate	65%	Good
Shrub Nester	10%	Good

Appendix C. Index of Biotic Integrity (IBI) for each site (if the park has multiple sites). Please refer to the Introduction for some important caveats pertaining to the IBI (continued).

2008   Acadia National Park - Seal Cove Center

Integrity Element: *Compositional*

Response Guild	Percentage	Rating
Exotic	0%	Good
Nest Predator / Brood Parasite	8%	Good
Resident	42%	Sig Concern
Single Brooded	63%	Caution

Integrity Element: *Functional*

Response Guild	Percentage	Rating
Bark Prober	13%	Good
Ground Gleaner	13%	Good
High Canopy Forager	8%	Caution
Low Canopy Forager	25%	Good
Omnivore	21%	Good

Integrity Element: *Structural*

Response Guild	Percentage	Rating
Canopy Nester	42%	Good
Forest-ground Nester	13%	Caution
Interior Forest Obligate	54%	Good
Shrub Nester	17%	Good

2007   Acadia National Park - Seal Cove East

Integrity Element: *Compositional*

Response Guild	Percentage	Rating
Exotic	0%	Good
Nest Predator / Brood Parasite	12%	Caution
Resident	36%	Caution
Single Brooded	52%	Caution

Integrity Element: *Functional*

Response Guild	Percentage	Rating
Bark Prober	8%	Caution
Ground Gleaner	12%	Good
High Canopy Forager	12%	Caution
Low Canopy Forager	20%	Caution
Omnivore	36%	Caution

Integrity Element: *Structural*

Response Guild	Percentage	Rating
Canopy Nester	44%	Good
Forest-ground Nester	12%	Caution
Interior Forest Obligate	48%	Good
Shrub Nester	16%	Good

2008   Acadia National Park - Seal Cove East

Integrity Element: *Compositional*

Response Guild	Percentage	Rating
Exotic	0%	Good
Nest Predator / Brood Parasite	11%	Caution
Resident	41%	Caution
Single Brooded	59%	Caution

Integrity Element: *Functional*

Response Guild	Percentage	Rating
Bark Prober	11%	Good
Ground Gleaner	7%	Caution
High Canopy Forager	11%	Caution
Low Canopy Forager	26%	Good
Omnivore	33%	Caution

Integrity Element: *Structural*

Response Guild	Percentage	Rating
Canopy Nester	41%	Good
Forest-ground Nester	7%	Caution
Interior Forest Obligate	44%	Good
Shrub Nester	26%	Sig Concern

2007   Marsh-Billings-Rockefeller National Historical Park - East

Integrity Element: *Compositional*

Response Guild	Percentage	Rating
Exotic	0%	Good
Nest Predator / Brood Parasite	10%	Caution
Resident	30%	Caution
Single Brooded	60%	Caution

Integrity Element: *Functional*

Response Guild	Percentage	Rating
Bark Prober	23%	Good
Ground Gleaner	7%	Caution
High Canopy Forager	13%	Good
Low Canopy Forager	13%	Sig Concern
Omnivore	30%	Caution

Integrity Element: *Structural*

Response Guild	Percentage	Rating
Canopy Nester	27%	Caution
Forest-ground Nester	20%	Good
Interior Forest Obligate	50%	Good
Shrub Nester	20%	Caution

Appendix C. Index of Biotic Integrity (IBI) for each site (if the park has multiple sites). Please refer to the Introduction for some important caveats pertaining to the IBI (continued).

2008　Marsh-Billings-Rockefeller National Historical Park - East

Integrity Element:　*Compositional*

Response Guild	Percentage	Rating
Exotic	0%	Good
Nest Predator / Brood Parasite	13%	Caution
Resident	29%	Caution
Single Brooded	58%	Caution

Integrity Element:　*Functional*

Response Guild	Percentage	Rating
Bark Prober	17%	Good
Ground Gleaner	13%	Good
High Canopy Forager	17%	Good
Low Canopy Forager	13%	Sig Concern
Omnivore	25%	Good

Integrity Element:　*Structural*

Response Guild	Percentage	Rating
Canopy Nester	38%	Good
Forest-ground Nester	8%	Caution
Interior Forest Obligate	46%	Good
Shrub Nester	17%	Good

2007　Marsh-Billings-Rockefeller National Historical Park - Northwest

Integrity Element:　*Compositional*

Response Guild	Percentage	Rating
Exotic	0%	Good
Nest Predator / Brood Parasite	10%	Good
Resident	32%	Caution
Single Brooded	55%	Caution

Integrity Element:　*Functional*

Response Guild	Percentage	Rating
Bark Prober	16%	Good
Ground Gleaner	13%	Good
High Canopy Forager	13%	Good
Low Canopy Forager	16%	Caution
Omnivore	32%	Caution

Integrity Element:　*Structural*

Response Guild	Percentage	Rating
Canopy Nester	39%	Good
Forest-ground Nester	13%	Caution
Interior Forest Obligate	48%	Good
Shrub Nester	13%	Good

2008   Marsh-Billings-Rockefeller National Historical Park - Northwest

Integrity Element: *Compositional*

Response Guild	Percentage	Rating
Exotic	0%	Good
Nest Predator / Brood Parasite	12%	Caution
Resident	36%	Caution
Single Brooded	60%	Caution

Integrity Element: *Functional*

Response Guild	Percentage	Rating
Bark Prober	16%	Good
Ground Gleaner	8%	Caution
High Canopy Forager	16%	Good
Low Canopy Forager	12%	Sig Concern
Omnivore	32%	Caution

Integrity Element: *Structural*

Response Guild	Percentage	Rating
Canopy Nester	40%	Good
Forest-ground Nester	16%	Caution
Interior Forest Obligate	40%	Good
Shrub Nester	20%	Caution

2007   Marsh-Billings-Rockefeller National Historical Park - South

Integrity Element: *Compositional*

Response Guild	Percentage	Rating
Exotic	0%	Good
Nest Predator / Brood Parasite	6%	Good
Resident	25%	Good
Single Brooded	56%	Caution

Integrity Element: *Functional*

Response Guild	Percentage	Rating
Bark Prober	13%	Good
Ground Gleaner	6%	Caution
High Canopy Forager	13%	Good
Low Canopy Forager	13%	Sig Concern
Omnivore	34%	Caution

Integrity Element: *Structural*

Response Guild	Percentage	Rating
Canopy Nester	41%	Good
Forest-ground Nester	16%	Caution
Interior Forest Obligate	31%	Caution
Shrub Nester	19%	Caution

Appendix C. Index of Biotic Integrity (IBI) for each site (if the park has multiple sites). Please refer to the Introduction for some important caveats pertaining to the IBI (continued).

2008   Marsh-Billings-Rockefeller National Historical Park - South

Integrity Element: *Compositional*

Response Guild	Percentage	Rating
Exotic	0%	Good
Nest Predator / Brood Parasite	4%	Good
Resident	22%	Good
Single Brooded	52%	Caution

Integrity Element: *Functional*

Response Guild	Percentage	Rating
Bark Prober	7%	Caution
Ground Gleaner	7%	Caution
High Canopy Forager	15%	Good
Low Canopy Forager	22%	Good
Omnivore	33%	Caution

Integrity Element: *Structural*

Response Guild	Percentage	Rating
Canopy Nester	41%	Good
Forest-ground Nester	11%	Caution
Interior Forest Obligate	33%	Caution
Shrub Nester	30%	Sig Concern

2007   Minute Man National Historical Park - Hartwell Tavern

Integrity Element: *Compositional*

Response Guild	Percentage	Rating
Exotic	0%	Good
Nest Predator / Brood Parasite	12%	Caution
Resident	42%	Sig Concern
Single Brooded	46%	Sig Concern

Integrity Element: *Functional*

Response Guild	Percentage	Rating
Bark Prober	19%	Good
Ground Gleaner	4%	Sig Concern
High Canopy Forager	8%	Caution
Low Canopy Forager	12%	Sig Concern
Omnivore	46%	Caution

Integrity Element: *Structural*

Response Guild	Percentage	Rating
Canopy Nester	31%	Caution
Forest-ground Nester	4%	Sig Concern
Interior Forest Obligate	19%	Caution
Shrub Nester	27%	Sig Concern

2008 Minute Man National Historical Park - Hartwell Tavern

Integrity Element: *Compositional*

Response Guild	Percentage	Rating
Exotic	0%	Good
Nest Predator / Brood Parasite	11%	Caution
Resident	29%	Caution
Single Brooded	36%	Sig Concern

Integrity Element: *Functional*

Response Guild	Percentage	Rating
Bark Prober	11%	Caution
Ground Gleaner	7%	Caution
High Canopy Forager	7%	Caution
Low Canopy Forager	14%	Caution
Omnivore	46%	Caution

Integrity Element: *Structural*

Response Guild	Percentage	Rating
Canopy Nester	14%	Caution
Forest-ground Nester	4%	Sig Concern
Interior Forest Obligate	11%	Caution
Shrub Nester	43%	Sig Concern

2007 Minute Man National Historical Park - Miriam's Corner

Integrity Element: *Compositional*

Response Guild	Percentage	Rating
Exotic	4%	Caution
Nest Predator / Brood Parasite	11%	Caution
Resident	39%	Caution
Single Brooded	39%	Sig Concern

Integrity Element: *Functional*

Response Guild	Percentage	Rating
Bark Prober	14%	Good
Ground Gleaner	4%	Sig Concern
High Canopy Forager	0%	Sig Concern
Low Canopy Forager	14%	Caution
Omnivore	54%	Sig Concern

Integrity Element: *Structural*

Response Guild	Percentage	Rating
Canopy Nester	21%	Caution
Forest-ground Nester	7%	Caution
Interior Forest Obligate	21%	Caution
Shrub Nester	32%	Sig Concern

2008   Minute Man National Historical Park - Miriam's Corner

Integrity Element: *Compositional*

Response Guild	Percentage	Rating
Exotic	4%	Caution
Nest Predator / Brood Parasite	12%	Caution
Resident	31%	Caution
Single Brooded	42%	Sig Concern

Integrity Element: *Functional*

Response Guild	Percentage	Rating
Bark Prober	8%	Caution
Ground Gleaner	8%	Caution
High Canopy Forager	12%	Caution
Low Canopy Forager	12%	Sig Concern
Omnivore	46%	Caution

Integrity Element: *Structural*

Response Guild	Percentage	Rating
Canopy Nester	27%	Caution
Forest-ground Nester	4%	Sig Concern
Interior Forest Obligate	12%	Caution
Shrub Nester	35%	Sig Concern

2007   Minute Man National Historical Park - The Bluff

Integrity Element: *Compositional*

Response Guild	Percentage	Rating
Exotic	8%	Sig Concern
Nest Predator / Brood Parasite	12%	Caution
Resident	46%	Sig Concern
Single Brooded	27%	Sig Concern

Integrity Element: *Functional*

Response Guild	Percentage	Rating
Bark Prober	15%	Good
Ground Gleaner	4%	Sig Concern
High Canopy Forager	4%	Sig Concern
Low Canopy Forager	15%	Caution
Omnivore	46%	Caution

Integrity Element: *Structural*

Response Guild	Percentage	Rating
Canopy Nester	19%	Caution
Forest-ground Nester	0%	Sig Concern
Interior Forest Obligate	8%	Sig Concern
Shrub Nester	31%	Sig Concern

2008   Minute Man National Historical Park - The Bluff

Integrity Element: *Compositional*

Response Guild	Percentage	Rating
Exotic	4%	Caution
Nest Predator / Brood Parasite	13%	Caution
Resident	38%	Caution
Single Brooded	38%	Sig Concern

Integrity Element: *Functional*

Response Guild	Percentage	Rating
Bark Prober	13%	Good
Ground Gleaner	0%	Sig Concern
High Canopy Forager	8%	Caution
Low Canopy Forager	8%	Sig Concern
Omnivore	46%	Caution

Integrity Element: *Structural*

Response Guild	Percentage	Rating
Canopy Nester	25%	Caution
Forest-ground Nester	0%	Sig Concern
Interior Forest Obligate	13%	Caution
Shrub Nester	33%	Sig Concern

2008   Morristown National Historical Park - Mt. Kemble

Integrity Element: *Compositional*

Response Guild	Percentage	Rating
Exotic	0%	Good
Nest Predator / Brood Parasite	6%	Good
Resident	34%	Caution
Single Brooded	37%	Sig Concern

Integrity Element: *Functional*

Response Guild	Percentage	Rating
Bark Prober	14%	Good
Ground Gleaner	9%	Caution
High Canopy Forager	6%	Sig Concern
Low Canopy Forager	11%	Sig Concern
Omnivore	40%	Caution

Integrity Element: *Structural*

Response Guild	Percentage	Rating
Canopy Nester	20%	Caution
Forest-ground Nester	11%	Caution
Interior Forest Obligate	20%	Caution
Shrub Nester	26%	Sig Concern

2007 Morristown National Historical Park - Primrose Brook

Integrity Element: *Compositional*

Response Guild	Percentage	Rating
Exotic	0%	Good
Nest Predator / Brood Parasite	10%	Caution
Resident	33%	Caution
Single Brooded	43%	Sig Concern

Integrity Element: *Functional*

Response Guild	Percentage	Rating
Bark Prober	13%	Good
Ground Gleaner	10%	Good
High Canopy Forager	7%	Sig Concern
Low Canopy Forager	13%	Sig Concern
Omnivore	33%	Caution

Integrity Element: *Structural*

Response Guild	Percentage	Rating
Canopy Nester	23%	Caution
Forest-ground Nester	17%	Caution
Interior Forest Obligate	27%	Caution
Shrub Nester	20%	Caution

2008 Morristown National Historical Park - Primrose Brook

Integrity Element: *Compositional*

Response Guild	Percentage	Rating
Exotic	0%	Good
Nest Predator / Brood Parasite	9%	Good
Resident	26%	Good
Single Brooded	48%	Sig Concern

Integrity Element: *Functional*

Response Guild	Percentage	Rating
Bark Prober	13%	Good
Ground Gleaner	9%	Caution
High Canopy Forager	13%	Good
Low Canopy Forager	0%	Sig Concern
Omnivore	48%	Caution

Integrity Element: *Structural*

Response Guild	Percentage	Rating
Canopy Nester	30%	Caution
Forest-ground Nester	13%	Caution
Interior Forest Obligate	22%	Caution
Shrub Nester	22%	Caution

2007   Morristown National Historical Park - Soldier's Huts

Integrity Element: *Compositional*

Response Guild	Percentage	Rating
Exotic	0%	Good
Nest Predator / Brood Parasite	12%	Caution
Resident	19%	Good
Single Brooded	54%	Caution

Integrity Element: *Functional*

Response Guild	Percentage	Rating
Bark Prober	12%	Good
Ground Gleaner	12%	Good
High Canopy Forager	12%	Caution
Low Canopy Forager	8%	Sig Concern
Omnivore	42%	Caution

Integrity Element: *Structural*

Response Guild	Percentage	Rating
Canopy Nester	31%	Caution
Forest-ground Nester	19%	Good
Interior Forest Obligate	31%	Caution
Shrub Nester	23%	Caution

2007   Saratoga National Historical Park - Middle Ravine

Integrity Element: *Compositional*

Response Guild	Percentage	Rating
Exotic	0%	Good
Nest Predator / Brood Parasite	8%	Good
Resident	28%	Good
Single Brooded	50%	Caution

Integrity Element: *Functional*

Response Guild	Percentage	Rating
Bark Prober	8%	Caution
Ground Gleaner	11%	Good
High Canopy Forager	6%	Sig Concern
Low Canopy Forager	14%	Sig Concern
Omnivore	44%	Caution

Integrity Element: *Structural*

Response Guild	Percentage	Rating
Canopy Nester	25%	Caution
Forest-ground Nester	11%	Caution
Interior Forest Obligate	22%	Caution
Shrub Nester	25%	Sig Concern

2008   Saratoga National Historical Park - Middle Ravine

Integrity Element: *Compositional*

Response Guild	Percentage	Rating
Exotic	0%	Good
Nest Predator / Brood Parasite	10%	Good
Resident	32%	Caution
Single Brooded	45%	Sig Concern

Integrity Element: *Functional*

Response Guild	Percentage	Rating
Bark Prober	13%	Good
Ground Gleaner	6%	Caution
High Canopy Forager	6%	Sig Concern
Low Canopy Forager	13%	Sig Concern
Omnivore	45%	Caution

Integrity Element: *Structural*

Response Guild	Percentage	Rating
Canopy Nester	23%	Caution
Forest-ground Nester	13%	Caution
Interior Forest Obligate	23%	Caution
Shrub Nester	23%	Caution

2008   Saratoga National Historical Park - Wilkinson Trail

Integrity Element: *Compositional*

Response Guild	Percentage	Rating
Exotic	0%	Good
Nest Predator / Brood Parasite	5%	Good
Resident	29%	Caution
Single Brooded	50%	Caution

Integrity Element: *Functional*

Response Guild	Percentage	Rating
Bark Prober	13%	Good
Ground Gleaner	3%	Sig Concern
High Canopy Forager	8%	Caution
Low Canopy Forager	13%	Sig Concern
Omnivore	37%	Caution

Integrity Element: *Structural*

Response Guild	Percentage	Rating
Canopy Nester	24%	Caution
Forest-ground Nester	13%	Caution
Interior Forest Obligate	26%	Caution
Shrub Nester	32%	Sig Concern

2008   Saratoga National Historical Park - Bemis Heights

Integrity Element: *Compositional*

Response Guild	Percentage	Rating
Exotic	0%	Good
Nest Predator / Brood Parasite	11%	Caution
Resident	29%	Caution
Single Brooded	57%	Caution

Integrity Element: *Functional*

Response Guild	Percentage	Rating
Bark Prober	11%	Caution
Ground Gleaner	4%	Sig Concern
High Canopy Forager	11%	Caution
Low Canopy Forager	14%	Caution
Omnivore	36%	Caution

Integrity Element: *Structural*

Response Guild	Percentage	Rating
Canopy Nester	25%	Caution
Forest-ground Nester	18%	Caution
Interior Forest Obligate	25%	Caution
Shrub Nester	29%	Sig Concern

NPS D-57 May 2009

www.ingramcontent.com/pod-product-compliance
Lightning Source LLC
Chambersburg PA
CBHW081118290526
45795CB00006B/2163